Praise for RESURRECTING VENUS

"*Resurrecting Venus* will draw you in and forever change the way you view being a woman. Cynthia masterfully explains that any movement to liberate and empower women must include embracing our feminine strengths. This wonderful guide is filled with practical approaches to becoming confident, attracting a solid romance, creating financial abundance, raising emotionally healthy children, and taking ownership of your inherent beauty. Give this book to every woman you know."

—Wendy Ida, Author of *Take Back Your Life!*

"Cynthia Occelli and I have been friends for over a decade. She has a spirit of peace that I saw severely tested by a tumultuous and painful journey. I have never seen anyone come through such difficulty with so much grace, calm, and excitement about life. Whenever I'm feeling overwhelmed, I pray, and then I talk to Cynthia. She has a way of seeing through all the 'stuff' and getting right to the core of what's going on. With a gentle hand and listening ear, she's able to help me navigate my way back to sanity.

"Cynthia often talks to me about enjoying life, taking care of myself, and reveling in my femininity. In a 'dog eat dog' world, she has shown me by example that it's okay, even empowering, to use the unique gifts that God gave us as women to live our dreams and fulfill our life purpose. Cynthia can tap into chaos and negative emotions and come away with a clear understanding of how to overcome those challenges. I love my friend, and I thank God for her."

—Sherri Shepherd, comedienne, actress, co-host of *The View*, author of *Permission Slips: Every Woman's Guide to Giving Yourself a Break*

"In language both eloquent and direct, *Resurrecting Venus* takes us into the depths of the feminine essence in its earthy and mystical aspects. Cynthia echoes a time when the truths she shares prevailed on the planet, when the gifts of the divine feminine were fully recognized and flourished to the profound benefit of all sentient beings. She reminds us that honoring the feminine or Shakti principle of life force is, in fact, the key to healing not only individual wounds, but also the woundedness of the world at large. A must read for women and men alike."

—Michael Bernard Beckwith, Author of *Life Visioning*

"Finally, a woman who understands men! Cynthia decodes the minds and motivations of men and gives women a clear approach to inspiring us to give them our all. She's living proof that the most powerful women are those who embrace their feminine strengths. *Resurrecting Venus* is pure genius; every single woman alive should read it and celebrate."

—Tony Berkman, CEO, Blog Catalog

"I loved reading every word. Cynthia's writing is captivating. She brilliantly explains how all women, from homemakers to high-level executives, can use their feminine power to create fulfilling lives and that being a powerful woman doesn't mean behaving like a man. She courageously reveals her own mistakes and heart-rending tragedies as a means for giving hope to all 'sisters' and helping us make better choices. *Resurrecting Venus* is incredibly inspiring!"

—Shelly Lefkoe, Co-founder, Lefkoe Institute & Author of *Parenting the Lefkoe Way*

"*Resurrecting Venus* is a call for all women to more deeply awaken to who we are and let our healing power bring positive change to our planet. With true stories and timeless wisdom, Cynthia lovingly shows us how to fill our hearts, so we can transform our lives and the lives of others."

—Agapi Stassinopoulos, Author of *Unbinding the Heart*

"*Resurrecting Venus* speaks to generations of women and unlocks the mystery of how to be feminine while remaining in your power. Cynthia takes you on a journey of personal transformation and an exploration of love, sisterhood, grace, and beauty. She embodies modern-day Venus and will connect you to your inner goddess. Read this book!"

—Latham Thomas, Author of *Mama Glow: A Hip Guide to Your Fabulous Abundant Pregnancy*

"*Resurrecting Venus* is a must read for any person, especially women who have been subjected to the denial and abuse of the feminine, including Mother Earth, and are now ready to fully grasp and actualize their true, divine nature. This book is wonderfully written and so very personal and practical."

—Dr. Terry Cole-Whittaker, Author of *What You Think of Me is None of My Business*

RESURRECTING
VENUS

ALSO BY CYNTHIA OCCELLI

Guided Meditation for Beginners

Guided Meditation for Self Worth

Guided Meditation for Prosperity

Inspired Living

CYNTHIA OCCELLI

RESURRECTING
VENUS

A Woman's Guide to
Love, Work, Motherhood,
& Soothing the Sacred Ache

Embrace
Your
Feminine
Power

Agape Media International

Los Angeles, California

Published by Agape Media
International, LLC
5700 Buckingham Parkway
Culver City, California 90230
310.258.4401
www.agapeme.com

Distributed by Hay House, Inc.
P.O. Box 5100, Carlsbad, CA 92018-5100
760.431.7695 or 800.654.5126

Hay House USA: www.hayhouse.com®
Hay House UK: www.hayhouse.co.uk
Hay House Australia: www.hayhouse.com.au
Hay House South Africa: www.hayhouse.co.za
Hay House India: www.hayhouse.co.in

Cynthia Occelli
Resurrecting Venus

Content Editor: Robin Hoffman
Copy Editor: Jessica Bryan
Cover and Interior Design: Christy Collins
Photography: The Cheriefoto Team
Executive In Charge of Publication: Stephen Powers

Library of Congress Control Number: 2012948138

ISBN: 978-1-4019-4087-4

Printed in the USA on recycled paper.

SUSTAINABLE
FORESTRY
INITIATIVE
Certified Chain of Custody
Promoting Sustainable Forestry
www.sfiprogram.org
SFI-01268

SFI label applies to the text stock

A GIFT FOR YOU

Visit www.CynthiaOccelli.com/Venus to download

Embrace Your Feminine Spirit, a guided meditation, yours free.

"And the day came when the risk
to remain tight in a bud was more painful than
the risk it took to blossom."

−attributed to Anaïs Nin

For Aurora

CONTENTS

ACKNOWLEDGMENTS

Aurora, you are the light in my heart and the girl I always wanted to be. Thank you for choosing me.

To Robin, the boy I grew up with, thank you for giving me a reason to become my best. You are an extraordinary man.

To my mother, thank you for standing in the fires of searing opposition so we could stay together. I admire and adore you.

Lizzy, Brenda, and Oma, thank you and I love you.

Allan Glass, my hero, champion and rock, thank you for staying the course.

Rabab Koepp, my habibte, every woman should have a best friend as fiercely loving as you. Thank you for holding me together when everything fell apart.

Sherri Shepherd, thank you for always standing beside me and believing in my success.

Kathy Davis, thank you for telling me I'm beautiful all those years ago and showing me how to celebrate in the darkness.

Shelley Reid, thank you for your generosity, inimitable brilliance, and steadfast support. You inspire me.

Debra Whelan-Johnson, thank you for seeing the potential in me and giving me a chance.

Angelina Urquhart, my new friend who I've known forever, thank you for telling me I could do it.

Christine Fazzino thank you for always being my friend and making me laugh.

Reverend Cheryl Ward, thank you for standing up to my fears and seeing who I really am.

Margaret Richmond, thank you for loving me when I felt too small to matter.

Shelly Lefkoe, thank you for unbinding my wings.

Lisa Sparks Dettlaff, thank you for being my first fan.

Gigi Snyder, Ekaette Ekong, and Thomas Taubman, thank you for helping me stay on my mat as I wrote this book.

Tony Berkman, thank you for getting me "discovered."

Thank you to Stephen Powers and Michael Bernard Beckwith for creating the space and energy for my work to blossom.

Tristine Rainer, thank you for helping me capture my story.

Thank you to: Cherie Steinberg, Hedley Jones, and the whole Cheriefoto Team. Only you could grasp and create my vision of Venus.

I am deeply grateful to Robin Colucci Hoffman, my sister and developmental editor who gets it and gives everything she's got to make it great; Jessica Bryan, my fantastic copy-editor who sees the energy behind the words; and Christy Collins, my brilliantly talented book designer.

Thank you to the wonderful women of Hay House: Louise Hay, Margarete Nielsen, Gail Gonzales, and Richelle Zizian.

Finally, to my virtual sisters, your open hearts, loving support, and passionate challenges helped me write this book. Special thanks to: Mary Birmingham, Teresa Britton, Deb Crandell Bzdula, Shelli Clemens, Vasoulla Valerie Demetriou, Debi Dritchas, Janice Earls, Betsy Maxwell Foreman, Peggy Goodman, Nabanita Gupta Ghosh, Nicola Hay, Ruth Kotler, Lucy Loizou, Barbara Moran, Nicole Molière, Myra Naito, Elizabeth Peterson, Maria Rivera, Meredith Rose, Gretchen Spletzer, Diana Stackhouse, Jenifer Wheeler Walsh, Valli Ware, and Helen Worster. I am forever grateful.

PREFACE

My life had barely gotten started, and I'd already had enough. I was nineteen, a dropout, and a single mom living in a garage with my new baby. Staring at the rusted nails protruding from the rafters, I tried to make sense of what it meant to be a successful woman and what I'd have to do to become one. Before my son was born, success wasn't all that important to me. I wanted to be loved, have fun, and escape the uncomfortable monotony of life, but that time had ended. I was a mother now. I'd had plenty of examples of independent women who were living the life I was taught to want, but I knew too much of their inner suffering to believe they were genuinely happy. Success and happiness seemed to be opposing polarities. *If only I could find a way to bring them together.*

I grew up in the '70s and '80s, watching the women around me declare how happy they were with their power and independence. My mother, aunts, and their female friends all worked two jobs; polished their homes; raised children, and compensated for incompetent, or more often, absent, men. For them, happiness meant being in control. Hard work was the answer to every challenge. Success was paying the bills, competing with men, and exercising sexual freedom. They wore a mask of satisfaction and confidence, while suppressing any emotion that might be interpreted as weakness. They were a tough-looking crew on the outside, brandishing an approach-at-your-own-risk image, but if by some unguarded route you managed to infiltrate their fortress-like facades, you'd catch a glimpse of what was going on underneath.

As a sensitive and hyper-observant child, I slipped past their unmanned barriers often. Behind locked gates sat acres of forgotten gardens. Overgrown with thorny, serpentine vines encircling ornate iron fences, their dreams, desires, passions, romantic yearnings, spiritual needs, and life purposes were sewn to the sediment beneath decaying fallen leaves. Trapped and tied down, their feminine essences languished. Over time, I saw those repressed energies escape, frenzied and wounded, wreaking havoc in each woman's life. It seemed to me that women's hard-won advances in power and independence, though vital and valuable, had a direct and negative correlation with happiness. Later, studies would give credit to my suspicions.[1]

Determined to gain a chance at joyful living, I began my quest. As with all explorations of possibility, we first look to real-life examples. I turned to my grandmother's generation. Sitting with women born in the 1920s and 1930s, I listened to their stories. Most women of their generation were bred and born to become mothers and obedient wives, relegated to nurseries, PTA meetings, kitchens, and knitting rooms. Their dreams and passions were neatly tucked under lace doilies, pressed aprons, and freshly folded laundry. For most, an inexplicable longing tugged at their insides, much the way their children tugged at their skirts and apron strings. Some less-than-brilliant men labeled this insatiable and amorphous yearning "frigidity." Our grandmothers' gardens were frozen, and many never had the opportunity to thaw.

Still, according to recent research, women in our grandmothers' generation were far happier than many women are now. This may be true, but being more happy than miserable is a dubious goal.

I wanted to live with the inner joy I'd caught whispers of as a child. I wanted freedom, harmony, peace, love, abundance, and creativity. I wanted to live in celebration of life. I couldn't accept that this joyful experience only existed in the imagination of a child's wanderlust. I couldn't fathom living my entire adult life in varying shades of muted color. The power, freedom, and self-determination my mother and her peers fought for so valiantly were precious gifts, but they weren't enough to make a life—not the kind of life I wanted, anyway.

With the coals of my teenage rebellion still glowing, I threw out my mother's manifesto of womanly success along with all of society's rules and limitations, and the media's efforts to manipulate, manage, and control women. I resolved that, come what may, I would have it all, and the central piece of this "all" was the quality of joy I'd glimpsed as a child. I would not surrender my dreams or paint myself into a corner marked "female independence." Beyond happiness, I wanted health, radiant beauty, an education, success, a well-loved child, financial wealth, and a paradisiacal sanctuary to call home. And that wasn't all; I wanted to shine in my femininity.

I'd read books detailing the lives of history's most worshipped women and celebrated goddesses. Their beauty, power, kindness, and sometimes magical ability to create wonder in the world filled me with light, even in the darkest moments. I loved everything about being a woman, and the thought of repressing the glorious gifts of feminine grace in the name of independence, equality, or anything else made me ache.

Though I'd never known a man who wielded his masculine power with competence or compassion (my father was absent, my child's father was abusive and absent, and no man had ever loved me more than he loved possessing me), somewhere inside I knew that healthy, beautiful romance was real. I fantasized about reveling in love with a man so secure in his manhood that he could immerse himself in my sensuality without being overcome by fear or the urge to dominate me. He would be powerfully masculine, capable of loving me fiercely, and encouraging my need to soar. My desire grew so strong that I realized I'd rather be alone than in relationships with lesser men. I would not settle.

I knew everything about what I wanted and nothing about how to get it. I reasoned that at least I was clear on what I *didn't* want, and that had to count for something. The beautiful thing about starting from less than zero is that you have nothing to lose. I was already broke, uneducated, overweight, on welfare, and responsible for the most amazing little boy in the world. If everything I tried imploded, how much worse could it be? Other people didn't share my opinion. When I explained my vision of the life I intended to create, I received nothing but eye-rolls and concerned attempts to shake me from my obvious delirium. I became accustomed to hearing things like, "Get your feet on the ground," or "Accept reality." Looking back, I realize that I had already accepted the positive reality I'd envisioned. It just hadn't manifested yet.

Within five years of my decision to follow my heart's desires, my life bore no resemblance to its prior distressing state. I was beginning my second year of law school, a feat most had thought impossible, considering I'd dropped out of high school in ninth grade. I was running a successful real estate business, engaged to the man I'd imagined, and was building my sanctuary in Bel Air, California. I was thin, and for the first time in my life I felt beautiful. I even began to dabble in modeling and acting. I had become the complete expression of the feminine woman I'd longed to be. My unrealistic reality had manifested; I had it all.

Over the years, I've made grave mistakes; encountered tremendous challenges; suffered tragedy; and, against my essence, fought like a man. I'll share much of it with you. Throughout this book, I've included personal stories that serve to demonstrate the successful and unsuccessful ways of applying feminine power and essence. My early successes gave me the confidence to stand in the fire and know that the power within is greater than any challenge. When you finish this book, you'll know, too.

Resurrecting Venus was written for women who, at their essence, are feminine and want to strengthen their connection to their power and expression. Not all women are innately feminine. Some women are born with energetically masculine inner structures—just as there are men who are essentially feminine. These women, who bear shades of the Greek goddess Artemis, excel at delivering their magnificence to the world through intellect, force, and the hunt. Possessing a heightened level of masculinity, they generally choose relationships with others who are ruled more by femininity. This book may not appeal to innately masculine women; it may even incense them. I love and seek the best for all people, and it's my hope that you will look within for your essential energy and follow its lead.

How can you discern whether your essence is feminine? Some women know they are feminine as clearly as they know their own name. Many feel their feminine essence swirling beneath layers of acquired masculinity. In all of my years of working with women, the stirring desire to be feminine is a result of *being* essentially feminine because we are drawn to what we *are*. Some women are disconnected from their feminine essence or lack understanding of what femininity means. Consider the following questions to help you discern your essential energy.

What makes you happier:

* Being pursued by a lover or pursuing one?

* An emotional connection or healthy competition?

* Spending time in sisterhood or hanging out with a couple of male friends?

* A relationship with a man who will protect, provide for, and adore you or one who looks to you for leadership?

* Nurturing your children yourself or sharing the responsibility with many capable people?

* Reading a romance novel or building a machine or structure?

In each of these choices, the first option is one a woman with a primarily feminine essence is more likely to choose. The second option reflects a more masculine essence. You may be in the middle. Wherever you are is right for you. Follow your own truth, but know that this book was written specifically for the essentially feminine woman.

Resurrecting Venus is intended to serve the countless women who feel uninspired, unfulfilled, and disconnected from unconditional joy. For many years, I've helped women resurrect the Venus within, and I've witnessed powerful transformations from misery and mediocrity into magnificence. I know from real-world examples and experiences that you can have the life you ache to live. It's my heart's desire and dream to share all I know with you.

The Divine Feminine—represented here by the goddess Venus—is a loving, creative energy that heals, soothes, connects, enlivens, and manifests the desires of the heart. Women often erroneously confuse femininity with weakness. It's anything but weakness. Femininity is strength fueled by love.

Sometimes women feel uncomfortable openly acknowledging their yearning to embrace their femininity. They're afraid to be perceived as anti-feminist or backward-looking traitors to the ideals of the women's liberation movement. This mistaken belief blocks access to the life-righting power of feminine essence. Resurrecting Venus is never a betrayal. Women and men are entitled to equal rights, opportunities, and pay, and yet we are profoundly different.

No fear of political incorrectness justifies ignorance of the truth. It doesn't take research to know that women are capable of things men will never be able to do and that men have strengths we cannot match.

When you embrace your feminine essence, you'll discover an ocean of liquid inspiration, serenity, and creative power. The experience feels much like the first moments after waking from a wondrous dream. This exquisite feeling becomes your new normal. It's sublimely soothing, rife with deep joy, and wholly empowering.

When you connect with your feminine core—which can be found in the space a little below and behind your navel—you'll travel the path back to creation. This energetic center is the garden of the goddess and the seat of intuition, leading directly to your higher self. All you need to know can be discovered in this sacred space of dreams, creativity, inspiration, and magnificence. Your heart shines over this paradise like the sun, radiating its wisdom and energy. In this perfect place, all things are possible. The work of Resurrecting Venus begins with moving away from the ego-driven mind and returning to the garden beneath your heart's sun.

Resurrecting Venus in your life is a generous act with the power to transform the world. Feminine energy in its purest form nurtures all of creation for the highest good of all. Whereas masculine energy represents power, competition, and control (not inherently negative qualities), the feminine unites, cooperates, and supports. Many of the problems in the world can be traced to masculine energies running amok, unchecked and unbalanced by feminine energy. As women, when we embrace our feminine essence, we bring femininity to its rightful place: beside the masculine on the world's throne. However, if we are to reveal the feminine we wish to see in the world, we must first accept it within ourselves.

Cynthia Occelli

Bel Air, California

2012

NOTE

1. See Betsey Stevenson and Justin Wolfers's paper, "The Paradox of Declining Female Happiness" in the *American Economic Journal: Economic Policy 2009*, 1:2, 190-225

HOW TO READ THIS BOOK

Resurrecting Venus is written in a manner that reflects one of the most powerful feminine strengths: the ability to shape-shift to fit the needs of any situation. In some sections, you will hear the voice of your sweet and sassy best friend; others will sound like a no-nonsense mom; and some will tickle your ears with the croon of a sensual, passionate romantic.

Before I sat down to write, I would pray and meditate and call on the Divine Feminine. I asked that every expression coming through me would be for your highest good and communicated in a way that was clear and understandable, and that the information would call you to action, when necessary.

This book is both spiritual and practical. We are spiritual beings living in a physical universe, so we must live from love-based wisdom as well as practice sound reasoning. One requires the other. Don't check your common sense at the door. Open your heart, use your brain, and, as in every aspect of your life, think for yourself. Check my ideas against your own inner thoughts and feelings.

If something does not resonate with you, before you dismiss it, examine whether it's triggering an issue you want to work through, or if it challenges a limiting belief that does not serve you. If after this inquiry, you are certain an idea is not right for you, disregard it. Nothing is right for everyone, and one of your greatest strengths is to trust yourself.

This book is divided into five stand-alone parts with numbered sections that may be read in any order. That said, I recommend reading Section I, Venus Eclipsed, first because it explains the symptoms, consequences, and dangers of repressed femininity, and highlights the negative influence of social dogma and the media. You will learn about women, including myself, who have misused feminine power, and how sometimes the greatest threat to the welfare of women is the behavior of other women. This foundational section will support you in understanding the purpose, freedoms, and benefits of embracing your feminine powers.

Section II, Venus in Love, will guide you in creating and maintaining the passionate, delicious, romantic, and solid love relationship you deserve. We'll explore how to avoid landing in yet another sugarless romance, and detail the single most important step every woman must take before entering the dating arena. You'll learn to connect with your inner Venus and allow her to govern your romantic life. Attracting the Adonis of your dreams isn't by luck or coincidence. I'll show you how to conjure and magnetize a hero who will love and worship you. You will unlock the mystery of what ignites the heart, mind, and loins of relationship-minded men as they share in their own words what they want in a woman (it's not what you might think). I use examples of relationships gone right and wrong to help you create the love life you want. We'll explore the super-smart, non-moralistic, non-religious basis for avoiding sex without monogamy. Finally, you'll discover the inner workings, strengths, and gifts the fully expressed masculine man can bring, and how to love and inspire him to move the heavens in the name of love for you.

Section III, The Goddess Mother, explores the creative miracle of pregnancy and childbirth, and equips you with the information you'll need to protect yourself and your baby from commercial forces that interfere with this womanly domain. You'll discover your power to increase the love in your life and literally change the world by building strong, emotionally intimate connections with your children, as well as practical suggestions on how to create this bond. We'll explore the importance of staying home with young children and discuss what you can do when you can't stay home. We'll look at the challenges our children face growing up in the Internet age, and I'll give you some tools to bolster your child's success.

Section IV, Venus at Work, explains how to use your feminine gifts to create abundance and success as a mother, entrepreneur, and professional. It introduces the need to reframe how women measure career success. You'll discover how your financial picture is a reflection of your deepest beliefs, and learn the secrets to gaining higher pay and promotions without sacrificing your femininity. You will learn how to use masculine energy as a tool to increase your success, and how to use your feminine powers to forestall the backlash of being perceived as a bitch.

In this section, we'll explore the power of choosing to be a stay-at-home mom and how to make this time pay off in the future. Women who are returning to the workplace after child-rearing, or working for the first time after a divorce or another life change, will find practical advice. You'll learn how your innate abilities and creativity can be harnessed to catapult you into a fulfilling career and financial success.

Section V, Resurrecting Venus, is devoted to calling forth the goddess in you. I'll dispel the common myths women believe about themselves and the feminine, and replace them with empowering truths. You'll learn the life-changing benefits of intelligent forgiveness, surrendering victimhood, and standing in your feminine power. I will support you in healing old wounds, releasing what no longer serves you, and recognizing the Divine showing up *as you*. From this awareness, you'll understand that the unique purpose of your life and your deepest desires are inextricably entwined. You'll discover the life you were born to live.

It's my deepest honor, joy, and privilege to walk beside you on the journey to becoming the greatest expression of who you are. To connect with many of your exquisitely feminine sisters and with me, join my blog at www.cynthiaoccelli.com and our Facebook page at www.facebook.com/LIFEblog.

PART I
VENUS ECLIPSED

1

THE FEMININE DARK AGE

The battle was never between the sexes;
it has always been between humankind and fear.
Let us claim our power and rest the pendulum of change
at the place of fully expressed femininity.

I grew up in the afterglow of the feminist revolution. As a young girl, my favorite television show was *Wonder Woman*, a weekly series about a sublimely beautiful female super-heroine who went about saving the world wearing a bedazzling bathing suit and sexy red boots. Second to Wonder Woman was The Bionic Woman, a technologically enhanced pin-up who could kick the mess out of any man. The third show in my TV trifecta of female perfection was *Charlie's Angels*, a series featuring three supermodels saving the world and answering only to Charlie, a velvet-voiced sugar daddy who commanded them by speakerphone. Between segments, I fawned over the perfume commercial that featured a blond bombshell who shook and shimmied while transforming herself from mother to business woman to sex kitten. From the top of the slide in the playground, I shouted the words to my favorite song, "I'm Every Woman," sung by Chaka Khan.

Women's equality meant that a successful woman did everything men did, only better. She raised children, ran a household, always looked stunning, and felt perpetually aroused. The only thing that could make her perfect life better was to get naked with a man without any commitment.

The women who raised me were less enthusiastic about the media's image of female success. To them, absolute independence from men was the pinnacle of womanly achievement. Men were no longer leaders or providers, but optional accessories. Men were responsible for everything wrong with the world, especially for every atrocity against women. It was men who'd imprisoned women, keeping them as chattel or concubines for all of recorded history. After the sisterhood's valiant fight for freedom from male dominance, a woman's most traitorous act was to embrace her captors. The successful modern woman was wholly self-reliant; she did it all. Husbands and fathers became unnecessary. The new woman was, all in all, a better man.

The feminist movement of the 1960s and '70s missed the mark. It was less a feminist movement, and more a campaign to promote the systematic masculinization of women. In the frenzy to liberate women from male dominance, feminists still operated under the misperception that masculine is better than feminine. Some women continued to accept the experience locked into our language that "womanly" is synonymous with weak, flighty, conniving, and changeable, while "manly" means brave, bold, honorable, and effective.

Feminists continued to suppress and belittle the feminine by making their movement about how women should be more "like" men. The result: a missed opportunity to liberate the feminine and an ongoing, yet different, oppression of women. Still responsible for hearth and home, and still pressured to look "perfect," women now have secured for themselves the added burdens of being the breadwinner and often overseeing infantile male partners.

The fear of feminine power that spurred female oppression in the first place lives on. Modern society has only suppressed the expression of it. Men feel inadequate because nearly everything they do is belittled, criticized, or perceived as bungled. The incompetent, submissive airhead wives of 1950s TV fame have been replaced by the clueless, perpetually adolescent man-children of today's sitcoms and commercials. Women driven by the fear of anything less than absolute equality now diminish and oppress men, too.

In truth, the sexes are not, and never will be, the same. An obvious example is that men will never give natural birth and women, on average, will always be physically weaker than men. In this, and a myriad of other ways, we are different. We must stop confusing equality with sameness.

Our differences, when positively expressed, create a sublime power capable of supporting all people and healing the problems that plague our communities. After decades of living out the aftermath of the post-feminist revolution, women, men, and children are suffering. Mental-health costs and the use of antidepressants have skyrocketed. Women are busy, stressed, tired, and unhappy. The world as it is today—polluted, at war, drained of resources, and occupied by millions who are suffering—is a reflection of policies devoid of the life-sustaining feminine wisdom that even women have abandoned.

It's time for women to reclaim their true power and rest the pendulum of change at the place of fully expressed femininity. No one else can do this. The joy and fulfillment of the majority of women depend on it, as does the well-being of the world.

2

THE SACRED ACHE

No longer bound by myths,
mirages, and manipulations,
the woman who honors the sacred ache goes free.

If you are under the age of 50, chances are you learned that a happy woman is educated, employed, self-sufficient, financially independent; a hands-on mother, dutiful daughter, loyal friend, eager lover; and the "fix it" resource for every needy soul. No matter what your age, you probably accepted the belief that a woman thrives on giving far more than she receives, and everyone loves her for it. Droves of women labor for decades, valiantly striving to achieve this contrived ideal.

After achieving all they were taught to want, the few women who reach the "Promised Land" often crash in crisis. After decades of stress, self-sacrifice, and neglect, they're devastated by the realization that the feminist nirvana they were bred to pursue is a mirage. Being, doing, and having everything they were supposed to want brought more exhaustion than satisfaction. Something is still missing, but they haven't a clue what it is. At the same time, the stifling realization descends: to keep what they've struggled so hard to achieve, they must continue giving all they've got. They become slaves to the machine of their lives, or they must pay an extraordinarily high price to get out, often foregoing the status, money, and the little bit of emotional support they have managed to eke out of their significant relationships.

The way out of this dilemma is daunting, complicated, and financially and emotionally expensive. The society that duped them into believing that becoming Superwomen would make them happy has unapologetically let them down. Disheartened and numb, many women choose to resign themselves to a life of obligation, soothing their aching souls with food, romance novels, television, antidepressants, or worse.

The majority of modern women have cut off the flow of their own feminine energy and refused its healing and grace. Without the feminine strengths of compassion, abundance, and kindness ruling our hearts, we neglect and abuse ourselves. Like nomads wandering a desert of competition, dissatisfaction, and lack, we attempt to find solace in the masculine traits of force, aggressiveness, and dominance.

We work harder, worry more, manipulate, and criticize. We hide our beauty beneath masculine hairstyles and clothing, or we exaggerate our sexuality, further promoting exploitive and disempowering feminine stereotypes. Like roses drenched in seawater, we cannot thrive. Shriveled, parched, and desperate to blossom, our true selves waste away.

The detrimental consequences of disconnection from our feminine essence reach far beyond our individual lives. Without Venus, the goddess of femininity, living within us, the entire world suffers. It is our personal obligation, to each other and the world, to restore our feminine essence.

A woman enticed by the whispered knowing that there must be something more, something sublime and deeply fulfilling, often experiences what society may view as a break with "reality," or the popular and craftily titled term "midlife crisis." I prefer to call it the "birth of truth." It first arrives as an ache. This sacred ache, felt deep within, is a calling from our true selves imploring us to let go and live our purpose. It's the beginning of the realization that you will not accept a life sentence of being everything to everyone but yourself, and an awakening to the fact that you are here to express the gifts you were created to give. Though we may not immediately recognize the voice of our true self, when we choose to listen we realize it has always been there, waiting patiently to show us the way to heaven on earth. A few women are fortunate to feel the despairing ache for "something more" early in life; for others, the message is heard much later. It is, however, always a gift.

If you are like most women, you can remember a time in childhood when your essence overcame you. Whether through a whispering field of flowers, a glob of paint on the tip of a brush, the breath of a puppy, the feeling of dough in your hands, the wind whipping your hair as you raced down a grassy hill, or being lifted by the swelling waters of the sea, somewhere in time, something powerfully moved you. In those ineffable moments, logic gave way to fascination, joy, and revelry. It wasn't a random moment of insignificant pleasure. You were connected to your Source, your true self, your unique being, and to the soul of the world.

In perfect wisdom, our Creator endowed us with a natural attraction to our purpose. We are divinely designed to gravitate toward it, just as mothers of all species are irresistibly drawn to their young. A woman is not crafted with a passion to be a composer, yet destined to be an accountant. Our Creator is brilliant, not cruel. You were brought here to deliver the gifts you most adore to this world in a way that only you can. The most intelligent and loving choice you can make for yourself and all of creation is to heed this call.

In another stroke of formidable genius, our Source formed and infused women with femininity—a plethora of inherent strengths tailored to support and nurture the expression of our purpose. Once revered in ancient civilizations, our essential femininity is a womb perfectly designed to nurture the gifts, creations, and innate talents of every living thing. It gestates our deepest desires, translating energies into manifested outcomes and ensuring their survival in the physical world. No purpose is given without the means to achieve it.

Harmony, peace, and blissful growth are constants in a life lived from and guided by our feminine essence. Here, the ache of the unfulfilled feminine heart subsides. Each day is lived with the infinite support of the true self and unparalleled satisfaction emerges. When Source and the higher self and mind are aligned, all things are possible, and the life women were created to live begins.

When she is connected to her feminine essence, a woman blossoms in the abundant flow of creation. Motivated by kindness and a lust for the greater good, she knows that to embody the universal mother, she must first care for herself. Only then can she shine her light on her family, friends, and the world. Wisely, she puts herself first, taking the time required to honor her heart, body, and life. It's the most generous thing she can do.

When difficulties arise, the woman connected to her essence knows that the universe will conspire to help her if she remains true to herself. She does not become terrified, lost, or insecure. She trusts her intuition, stays open for guidance, and maintains faith in the power that designed her life-giving form. She exchanges the image of carrying the world on her shoulders for one of truth supported by grace.

3

THE DARK SIDE OF FEMININITY

A woman severed from her feminine essence
is lost in a sprawling wilderness.
With fear as her only companion,
the seeds of all manner of madness take root.

Pamela is a bitch and proud of it. She's been married and divorced twice, and has two grown children, a high-powered career, and a knack for bedding the richest guy in the room. She lives in a stunning penthouse, drives a car worth more than most homes, and hasn't seen a coach-class plane ticket since her first divorce. If you're a friend of Pamela's, you've got status, connections, fame, or something else she wants. Once she's gotten what she was after, you're tossed aside. If she deems you an enemy, may the gods be with you. If you're happily married, or richer or more beautiful than she is, you're an enemy.

Her breasts set on a platter under clothes that cling like a baby's skin, Pamela bulldozes her way through the most elite crowds. Everyone knows her, and no one trusts her. Ask her about love, and she'll tell you it doesn't exist: Get what you can, and move on before they do. Having loved twice and been burned, she's too smart for that now—a lesson she regularly shares with her children.

To someone who doesn't know her, Pamela appears extraordinarily successful. She's powerful and in control of her life. She's 150 percent independent, a fashionista, socialite, and world-traveler with everything you'd ever want—and then there's the truth.

Pamela is locked inside a self-made prison of repressed femininity. Women who believe that success is a product of emulating men lock an enormous source of power and strength away. They starve themselves of emotional intimacy, adoration, nurturing, and being nurtured. They bury the feminine strengths that give them a unique advantage in the world. As their material and sexual conquests multiply, they become more disconnected from love, the vital life force that soothes and heals.

Ever since Pamela concluded that, in a man's world, the key to success is to be a better man, she has systematically stripped her being of all things feminine or, as she defines it, weak. She chose a degree in business management despite her passion for architecture, married a man who would "hand her the pants," and took only 10 days of maternity leave from her 60-hour-a-week career to be with her newborn child.

When her husband (who was tired of living with a score-keeping roommate) fell in love with an emotionally feminine woman, her marriage failed. Convinced that he left because the mistress was sexier, Pamela lost 20 pounds and had her breasts, nose, and lips done. She doesn't look like herself anymore, and she doesn't look better.

Bitterness, jealousy, and suspicion are seamlessly woven into Pamela's mental landscape. To her, they're assets that protect and motivate her. When she feels sadness or the whispering ache for her feminine essence, she responds decisively, choking off the unwanted thoughts and reinforcing the belief that softness leads to annihilation. She's become so proficient at stifling every emotion that could lead to vulnerability that she no longer consciously feels anything resembling tenderness.

The difficult moments come when her defenses fail. When she drinks a little too much, heavy, irrepressible tears fall; she then calls her current best friend and shares things she regrets revealing in the morning. Frequently, she wakes up at night swirling in darkness, frightened and alone, even when someone is beside her. Her imprisoned feminine self, clawing and thrashing to escape, can only be subdued by prescription drugs.

Though Pamela's story may seem extreme, women everywhere believe it's the only way to survive in this world and strive to be just like her. Buying into the witless myth that a successful woman is emotionally disconnected, financially independent, and a high achiever who won't hesitate to put a man in his place, women disown their inherent strengths, opting for competition, dominance, and force, instead. The emergence of successful, albeit secretly miserable, women in modern society makes the myth seem true, and it spreads like a virus. As alcoholism, depression, anxiety, and anguish skyrocket, few seek out the source of the ills. Instead, they explore more ways to mask the symptoms and continue to act out the toxic farce.

By stifling the innately feminine drive to heal, unite, and nurture, women become critical, judgmental, and controlling. They're less compassionate and patient with themselves, too, judging self-care to be the equivalent of slacking off. Instead of choosing men who are eager to protect, honor, and provide for them, they pick men who become dependent or behave like rebellious adolescents. Believing that a strong, powerful woman must have a career, they deprive themselves of staying at home with their children, even though no profession requires more skill, tenacity, or brilliance than raising a child. Though the decisions these women make seem intelligent at the outset, any appearance of gain is sure to be surpassed by a harrowing backlash later when the pangs of unmet feminine needs surface.

The presence of feminine energy within is not a choice; it's a living force that moves within us whether we accept it or not. To deny, repress, or restrain this energy causes it to react in painful and sometimes cruel ways. Like saddling a lioness, it's as pointless as it is dangerous.

When competition and aggressiveness rule a woman's life, her imprisoned feminine energy festers, feeding on its own distress. The manifestations of suppressed femininity range from illness, depression, and weight gain to loss of the ability to be emotionally intimate and complete mental breakdown. The more repressed feminine energy is, the greater its negative expression.

Eventually, the prisoner of repressed femininity breaks free. In the best case, a woman claims her rightful place as sentient ruler of her life and mind. A new life, driven by the desires of her heart, emerges. Her truth is birthed into being. In less fortunate outcomes, the prisoner emerges angry, bitter, and resentful. She counts the years lost, and the toll her life has taken on her soul makes her boil. She is vicious, insensitive, and scorned. There is still a possibility that she will find a way to her own feminine truth and live its gifts, but there is no guarantee.

Languishing at the other pole of femininity's dark side are women who, contrary to Pamela, live from an extreme, distorted, and self-harming femininity. These women embrace the natural gifts of healing, caring, and nurturing others, but take them to a self-destructive extreme. Living doormats, they give endlessly, catering to relatives, children, friends, spouses, and their communities. They ignore their own desires and focus on making others happy. When asked about their personal goals and dreams, they have none for themselves; everything they do is for someone else. They have no boundaries and allow others to treat them disrespectfully.

Though she may be consciously unaware of her actions, a woman suffering under the weight of feminine martyrdom behaves like a victim. She feels she is less important than others, and she uses guilt to manipulate and get her way. She doesn't believe she matters or deserves to pursue her own happiness, and the world mirrors her beliefs. The martyred female considers it selfish to seek sexual satisfaction, honor and respect, or personal fulfillment. A slave to traditional views, she believes her place is at the beck and call of others, even though she resents them for it.

It's rare to discover a woman who has not experienced and expressed both poles of femininity's dark side at some point in her life. Families and societies relentlessly condition women and girls to repress their innate femininity to succeed in the world, and to over-express it when caring for others. Like butterflies in a field of dry flowers, women are starving for the nectar of the authentic feminine.

To be empowered, happy, and secure, a woman must rest firmly on the throne of femininity, confident in her value and her connection to Source. Unapologetically, she puts herself first, knowing that only when she is happy, nourished, and secure can she fulfill her purpose. Naturally endowed with qualities to attract and nurture her deepest desires, she balances the masculine energies in the world and her presence guides humankind toward peace and compassion.

4

THE FALL OF MAN

No longer exiled, man returns.
Taking the earth upon his shoulders,
woman is freed from enslavement.

Life with a fully evolved man is sublime. It allows a woman to live from her feminine essence and alleviates the burden of feeling she must do everything herself. A woman's commitment to equal rights, opportunity, and pay does not require her to haul groceries, do handyman work, mow the lawn, and father the children. It doesn't mean she has to be passionless, disinterested in juicy sex, or swap silk and lace for flannel. A woman can be a champion of female empowerment and still defer life's heavier, dirtier responsibilities to men. Many women, married women included, completely misunderstand this truth and unnecessarily grunt and grind through life. They've been taught to believe that a woman who supports gender equality must share in, or even take over, the tasks that the physically stronger sex (men) are innately better equipped to perform. Though it's vital to be able to take care of your needs if you must, when a capable man is present, doing the dirty work is an added burden that women need not assume. Few women derive a sense of accomplishment from performing manual labor. Even fewer feel comfortable asking the yearning question, "Where have all the burden-lifters, protectors, providers, fathers, and sexual worshippers gone?"

Throughout history, men have been both celebrated and reviled for their masculinity. There is no question that many of them have taken their inherent desire for success, power, and sex to deadly and disgusting extremes. Yet, especially when it comes to men, significant and valuable masculine qualities of centuries past are overlooked.

At one time, the masculine man had a single motivation: to protect, preserve, and provide for the people who depended on him. He gained recognition, fulfillment, and emotional satisfaction from succeeding in this endeavor. A man competent in these areas was a respected leader in his community. He felt a sense of purpose in doing well. He worked hard, because being productive was an inextricable part of demonstrating his worth. It mattered to him that his children, at least his sons, carry his family name forward with honor and become self-reliant. To that end, he remained physically present in their lives and provided for them. He took pride in his work, knowing it was a reflection of his character. He may have been involved with many women, often to the chagrin of his wife, but if he was fortunate enough to find real love, it fed his soul and fueled his success. He was a hero, a warrior, and a protector who needed to be needed.

Left to rule the world unopposed, many men also visited unimaginable violence, harm, and destruction on women, weaker groups of people, and the environment. Extreme manifestations of dominant masculine energies still threaten cataclysmic ruin in the world. All people, men and women, deserve equal rights, opportunity, freedom, and pay. These are basic, fundamental human rights. Without feminine caring to balance masculine drive, loss and harm are certain.

The women's liberation movement brought much-needed light to this darkened corner of humanity. In the Western world, women gained control of their bodies, sexual expression, and familial decisions. Feminist leaders cleared the way for high-level education, careers, and political leadership by and for women. The gifts our mothers and grandmothers bestowed upon us are invaluable and deserve our unceasing acknowledgment, appreciation, and gratitude.

Yet, as is consistent with all major societal shifts, the pendulum of change swung too far. Determined to prove we could do anything a man could do, as good as or better than a man, women chose to supplant men. They took control and became assertive, dominant, and decisive. They cut their hair, disguised their curves, and distanced themselves from the stigma of femininity. Taking on multiple societal roles, many women became both mother and father to their children.

Masculinity in men was demonized and ridiculed as overbearing and oppressive. Gentlemanly actions such as opening doors, paying for a meal, or lingering to allow a woman to exit an elevator first were twisted and interpreted as patronizing insults. At home, men became chauvinists if they didn't prepare an equal amount of bottles, change the same number of diapers, share in the cooking, or fold laundry. A "good man" performed traditionally female activities.

Blindsided and eager to avoid ostracism, the majority of men responded by amplifying their feminine qualities. They left their posts as leaders, protectors, and providers. Some men were content to be relieved of their former duties and embraced a perpetual youth, free and unencumbered with the old role of provider and its responsibilities. Others morphed into an energetically neutral balance of femininity and masculinity, suppressing their inner fires.

Most men fell silent, not knowing how to be true to their nature without condemnation. They became tentative and unsure, feeding the new perception that men weren't special and had nothing unique to offer women beyond sperm donations. No longer the cornerstone of their families, men became optional and often burdensome accessories.

The media heavily reinforced this notion by creating advertising and programming that portrayed men as either incompetent, bumbling buffoons or perpetually aroused adolescents. This tragic mischaracterization spread widely. Women responded by expressing their disdain for troublesome men and disappointment over the dearth of desirable ones. Suddenly a hero without a cause, men fell into a fragmented and smoldering silence. Their sons were born into a confused world and encouraged to become gender-neutral, and often their fathers, now devalued exiles, were absent.

Angry and confused, with no definable contributory role, some men opt to slake their raw thirst for sexual gratification in order to assert their masculinity. They use women for sex, avoid intimacy and commitment, and swap out partners like dirty socks. To them, women are competitive manipulators who can never be trusted.

Though the idea of a population with balanced masculine and feminine energies spread evenly across both genders appears desirable on the surface, it is deeply flawed. As men and women move further to the center of the masculine/feminine continuum, the polarities required to create and sustain sexual attraction diminish. For women who want passion, romance, and adoration, this dynamic fails them. Romantic passion between any two people (including same-sex couples) requires both masculine and feminine polarities. Without these opposite poles, relationships falter and fail, or, at best, progress as lukewarm, bonded companionships with romantic/sexual connections akin to a warm hug.

Though much has changed in the world of relationships, the hearts and souls of men remain intact. The hero lives. I've spoken with hundreds of men who—despite concern that their comments may attract criticism—shared their deep desire to return to the throne as strong providers, passionate lovers, and unapologetic achievers. Here are some of their insights:

"There are times when women need to be true to their life force. The feminine nature is beauty and, in some ways, chaos. Men are masculine, and by their nature they are driven to achieve things. It does no good for a masculine man to have a woman who comes home from work and acts like a man. It also does no good for a woman to have a man who can't make decisions and doesn't have a purpose."

"It was a great first step to gain equality in all realms of business and sports. Yet, as a man, I believe that given women bring life into this world, in many ways they are far stronger than any man. A woman today can do everything a man can do, plus give life. It will be an amazing world when women can be strong and lead from their feminine qualities instead of imitating a masculine way of being."

"Equality doesn't mean we are the same. It means equality!

"Equal rights, equal pay, equal opportunities....

"Women becoming masculine and men becoming feminine undermines both sexes and our society, and well, look around and that's what you see."

"We're all kind of lost men these days. A man can't stand up and do the things he's good at without causing flack, and he's criticized for not doing it, too. I want my daughter to know how to handle her life as a single woman, but also be secure enough to let a man care for her when she's married and a mother."

"As a man, I feel that men in today's society have lost their way. In an effort to allow women 'equality,' many men have shrunk back into the shadows afraid to be…well…men. Okay, I'm sure I'm going to be slaughtered for that one! Please don't hear me wrong. I don't believe in the dominating man/submissive woman roles, but I do believe that we need to be true to who and what we are. I mean really, as a man, I love women. Not to say that I don't admire and respect strong, successful women, but when I'm alone with my wife (of 19 years) I want to be with her 'womanly, feminine' side not her 'strong business' side."

Men are innate champions, and they rise to the demands placed upon them. Let us call for their protection and restore honor to the roles of husband and father. Allowing our lover to care for us does not weaken us. By returning him to the throne beside us, we can rule together, balancing his force with our power and, in the process, restore romance, sexual chemistry, and emotional harmony to our lives.

It's time to rest the pendulum at a place of equal rights and opportunity, while nurturing our feminine strengths and honoring the magnificence of masculinity.

5

HONORING THE SISTERHOOD

When a woman honors a sister,
she honors herself and the whole of womankind.

When united under a common goal, women are unstoppable. We have the power to rule the world with compassion. Endowed with gifts for creating intimacy and connection and fostering communication, we are born hardwired to bond. Yet women continue to hold an attitude of competition toward one another. Beneath a mask of supportiveness and admiration, women invest disturbing amounts of energy in sizing up other women, making judgments, and comparing:

"She's fat, gorgeous, skinny, hideous, tacky, rich, trashy, etc. I'm more (or less) beautiful, ugly, or fashionable than she is."

Perhaps by offering a trite smile or feigned indifference, a woman won't have any awareness that she did any judging or comparing, but when the next woman shows up, she's at it again. The comparison game is maddening. All players lose sooner or later. There is always someone younger, older, richer, poorer, thinner, fatter, and so on. Every critique is an attack on the sisterhood and the inner self, sending self-loathing messages of inadequacy and lack.

Rarely, if ever, does a woman stop to consider the consequences of these silent contests. Often oblivious she's engaging in the game, she doesn't recognize that she is tacitly reinforcing media messages designed to indoctrinate women into believing they are inherently defective and must strive for some socially imposed image of perfection. She doesn't stop to think whether she would condone the thoughts she projects toward other women if someone were to hurl those same thoughts at her daughter.

Thoughts are a powerful force that dictate how we view the world. They carry energies that impact us in material ways. Critical, envious thoughts poison the spirit and harm all women. It's impossible to come together and birth a world of compassion, peace, and beauty while picking one another apart.

The game of one-upmanship is only part of the problem. Gossip, betrayals, and affairs with married men are also manifestations of a divided sisterhood. With regard to gossip, every woman has been both victim and perpetrator. No woman enjoys being mocked, ridiculed, or dissected behind her back. Yet the overwhelming majority of gossip about women is perpetuated by other women. Women everywhere partake in this vicious act against their sisters. They feed voraciously on the perils, dramas, and mistakes of others, including public figures, people from work, and others in their personal lives. Ironically, women gossip about women to bond with other women and to feel better about themselves. Naively, they believe they are somehow exempt, and that no one in their circle is gossiping about them. Is it any wonder that women aren't in their rightful place of leadership, ruling the world with fairness and decency, when most cannot sit at the table in their own home without assassinating another woman's character?

Resurrecting Venus means we can choose to reclaim our goddess nature and refrain from gossiping. As mothers, we can do more than tell our children: "If you don't have anything nice to say, say nothing." We can model positive behavior and break the gossiping habit that diminishes us all, and turn our focus to how alike we are. When we remember that we all make mistakes, fail, and cause ourselves pain and sadness, we can set our judgments aside and treat our sisters with compassion.

THE OTHER WOMAN

Perhaps the greatest harm to women caused by women is something (I'm sorry to admit) I know from experience, because I've been both the perpetrator and the victim. At age 22, when I met my second husband, he was married with two young children. We had an affair. I was fully aware of his status. I had plenty of excuses and justifications for my actions: he was rarely home, he wasn't in love, he was unfaithful, I wasn't the one married, the marriage was doomed to begin with, and if he hadn't cheated with me he would have with someone else. These deflections only served to shield me from the indisputable fact that I had turned on a sister, conspired to violate her union, partook in the breaking of her heart, and contributed to the destruction of her family. As a member of womankind, I should have had no part in it.

Women rule families and relationships. For as much as a man may desire sexual variety, it's women who ultimately allow affairs to happen. Women have the sole ability to shift an entire society toward stronger families. Refusing to take part in an affair with a married or otherwise committed man will not stop him from wanting to have an affair. However, insisting that he be available before getting involved sends a message: "Think before you act, and understand there are consequences. We women will not conspire to help you harm us."

Returning to my story, I was conceived from an affair between my adolescent mother and an adult man who already had a wife and five children. Infidelity and betrayal seemed normal to me. I cannot blame my mother for failing to teach me something she didn't understand either. The women she grew up with routinely betrayed one another. One cannot be held accountable for what they genuinely do not grasp. However, responsibility attaches the moment we understand what we're doing and its impact.

Mistresses do not destroy marriages alone; they are co-conspirators. Marriages lost to affairs were broken before any tryst occurred. It falls upon the husband to have the integrity to leave a marriage instead of cheat, but so long as women are willing to reward men who demonstrate poor character, it will continue.

FIRST WIFE, SECOND WIFE

Nowhere does the battle of woman against woman play out with more intensity or volatility than between first wife and second wife. If the first marriage ended because of an affair with the woman who became the second wife, the first wife may feel robbed of her marriage, social status, and often her financial security. Powerless to stop it, she may become aggressive and ma-nipulative. It's insensitive and callous to judge her for reacting to the relationship equivalent of being burned alive. As the first wife smolders in the painful ashes of her former life, she sees the new wife as a soulless monster responsible for it all.

Regardless of the cause of the dissolution, if the first mar-riage produced children, the original wife's maternal alarms may clang out of control because a woman she had no say in selecting now has intimate access to her children. At the same time, the new wife feels jealous and resentful of the first wife, who, despite the divorce, will always be the children's only *true* mother and continue her queen's reign on the throne as "the mother of his children."

It falls on the stepmother to stand aside and allow the needs of her stepchildren to come before her own. If this concept is untenable for her, she must not join the family. As a wise and responsible woman, she must choose to protect all young, whether biologically hers or not, and do her part to create a healing and nurturing world. This choice can be difficult, and it requires a woman to rise above her own insecurities. Yet when she manages to do this successfully, she creates a harmonious home where she is deeply loved and valued by all. These are the women who succeed.

Both women, for the good of all, must channel their upset into harmless outlets—such as journaling or counseling with psychologists or clergy—and refrain from arguments, gossip, and especially the temptation to carry the battle forward through the children. It might not be easy or fair, but women must do their best to keep peace once the bonds of sisterhood have become frayed.

MOTHER-IN-LAW AND DAUGHTER-IN-LAW

Mother-in-law/daughter-in-law relationships are often unnecessarily troubled. Some mothers feel threatened when their sons fall in love. They feel like they're losing their "baby" to another woman. A mother who refuses to see her son as a man hampers his attempts to become one. She must see herself as a steward and support the next generation of wives and children by raising and releasing her sons to be whole and available husbands and fathers.

By shifting her perception of her son from her "little boy" to an adult man, she can support him in fulfilling his role as a fully evolved man. She must allow him to be free and never place him in the position of having to choose between his love interest and his mother. A wise mother willingly stands aside and allows her son's woman to become the love-center of his world. In doing so, she strengthens and protects the inimitable bond between her and her adult child. She does not lose anything. She gains a daughter and harmonious access to her grandchildren.

Free of competition and resentment, a mother and daughter-in-law relationship can be extraordinary and wonderful. Women united within a family bring peace, healing, and strength to all its members. This is the sisterhood at its best.

So long as women focus on ways to separate and disparage one another, the world is damned to a motherless reign. Let us collectively call on men to be the lovers, husbands, and fathers we deserve and desire. Let us abandon catty competition, gossip, and betrayal. Divided we are mere bits of light, fragmented and scattered—united we are the prism through which heaven projects itself onto earth. As women, our power in the world is equivalent to the strength of our sisterhood.

6

HEALING THE
FEMININE MIND

Serene and untouched,
a woman's mind is the seat of paradise.
When the serpents of fear and insecurity
seek to invade, she rests firmly rooted in her Truth.
No evil shall enter.

By design, a woman's mind is complex. Innately gifted at managing several activities while perceiving loads of detailed information, we are masters of multitasking. Ask a woman about a lunch date she had this afternoon, and she can recall every detail with clarity, from the company to the curtains. She does not make an effort to take in all the information. It's just there. Her mind doesn't stop at perceiving the information. Every bit is gathered and assigned meaning.

As mature, feminine women, we possess the ability to examine and consider the information we receive and use discernment when assigning it meaning. Yet even women make mistakes sometimes. Perhaps a friend seems irritated on the phone, and you erroneously assume it's something you said or did that caused it. A woman squints at you, and you just know it's because you're wearing the most unflattering outfit of all time, when, in fact, the sun was in her eyes. Thankfully, instances like these are inconsequential and do not interfere with our sense of well-being.

The meanings we perceived as young girls can haunt us for a lifetime. Much of a girl's experience does not support the development of a healthy, mature, feminine mind. Like boys, girls receive a mixture of positive and negative messages from parents, teachers, and relatives. Unfortunately, the ability of the female mind to extrapolate and assign deep meaning to seemingly minor events and comments leaves a young girl especially vulnerable to suggestion. The natural feminine desire to feel safe and accepted, and to bond with others, can lead her into a dangerous mental trap from which she may never escape.

When I was a child, I learned that my birth was an unexpected and undesired surprise. Thereafter, my little mind found a way to tie every negative or neutral experience in my life to the belief that I didn't deserve to be here. When I walked into a class and the teacher didn't acknowledge me, I assumed it was because I was unwanted. In second grade, I gave a mandatory oral report while hiding behind the projector screen because I so strongly believed that I was not good enough to be seen. I spent the first decades of my life hiding.

It only takes the tiniest remark to instill a belief of inadequacy or inferiority in a little girl. A teacher says she's not good at something, a friend belittles her for being too heavy, a boy tells her she's ugly, a parent tells her she talks too much—any of these slights can plant the seed for a dark and twisted view of herself and allow it to flourish.

From the moment a girl is born, people comment on her appearance and make pronouncements on how she looks compared to other girls. If she happens to match the current social standard of beauty, she will develop pride in, and may even come to rely on, her looks, while feeling intellectually inferior if no one praises her mind. If she doesn't fit her community's standards of beauty or intellect, she quickly receives the clear message that she isn't as desirable as other girls. The message that she is a powerful being who was born to express her unique gifts only gets communicated if she is fortunate enough to be surrounded with conscious, mature, healthy adults.

Even before adolescence, the assault intensifies, as the deluge of unrestrained media messages fill her environment. They tell her she needs more makeup; shinier hair; bigger breasts; a smaller bottom; the newest fashions; and loads of soaps, shampoos, and perfumes just to be considered adequate.

Priming her to be an insatiable consumer, they tout a manufactured image of the "ideal" woman who works hard and raises children effortlessly, while maintaining a tight, trim figure and a perfect manicure. She is strong, independent, educated, and often the breadwinner. When she comes home from a long day's work, she's so eager to have sex with her man that she can barely keep her pants on. But wait, there's more! She's happy all of the time, too.

When a girl fails to live up to the media's standard, which she inevitably will, the advertisers stand at the ready to sell just the thing to fix her. The message is insidious and merciless. Most adult women remain oblivious to the fact that their standards of happiness and beauty aren't their own and unwittingly spread the same harmful messages to their own daughters.

The dire consequences of these mental assaults on women endure. Instead of living an empowered, fulfilling life, women remain in a prison with invisible bars, only becoming aware of their incarceration when they make the effort to step out. Feelings of failure and inadequacy permeate the female self-perception. We cannot feel happy, fulfilled, worthy, or safe, because there is always some missing piece in the ideal that we cannot find a way to master.

This low self-worth holds women back in every area of life. Believing that we are unworthy of abundance, success, and happiness, we cling to unhealthy relationships, refuse to ask for equal pay at work, and subject our bodies to starvation and mutilation—all in a futile effort to reach the unreachable "ideal," so at last we can feel accepted and safe.

If you were to ask me what constitutes a *real* feminist movement, I'd say it begins with healing the feminine mind. We have the power to foster a sense of "enough-ness" in our sisters and raise our daughters to be invulnerable to harmful messages. We can explore and identify all the ways we misunderstood and drew erroneous and limiting beliefs from our experiences. We can clean out the clutter of advertising chatter and discover firsthand that a mind filled with empowering beliefs and inspired thoughts is unlimited in its abilities. Free and in control of our own feminine genius, we can feel secure and able to make the sometimes difficult but soul-restoring choices necessary to take good care of ourselves and live our purpose.

If you choose to take this on, the realization of your inherent worth will take hold and you will notice encouraging thoughts arising within you. Your outer world will reflect your inner work. Opportunities to achieve your deepest desires will surface out of areas you've looked into many times before, yet found nothing. Like-minded people will sense your shift and be drawn to you. Instead of struggling and strong-arming yourself into taking action, your feminine power will flow and carry you in the direction of your good. When you encounter harmful beliefs and situations, the strength of your truths will shine and dissolve all darkness. You will be in possession of yourself.

PART II
VENUS IN LOVE

7
SWEET, JUICY ROMANCE

*In the exquisite moment, bathed in the warmth
of her lover's gaze, she surrenders to the wild Divine.
It ravishes her, taking nothing, giving everything.*

In recent years, passion and romance have taken on a negative
connotation; women assume they must give up companionship,
tenderness, and trust to enjoy sublime romantic passion. A relationship filled with radiant heat conjures images of torrid sex
with a "bad boy" who's a terrible life partner. The assumption is
that you can only have one or the other. Not so. You *can* have a
loving, emotionally intimate, secure relationship that sizzles.

Romantic passion between any two people (including same-
sex couples) requires a polarity of masculine and feminine
energies. A world of men and women with equally balanced
masculine and feminine energies may seem appealing on first
look, but it's poisonous to romance. As a feminine woman, you
desire passion, romance, and a sense of being protected and
adored (and why wouldn't you want this?). The energetically
neutered man, with an equal balance of masculine and feminine
energies, cannot sate your feminine desires. Your feminine essence—which yearns to be wrapped in the restrained strength
of a champion who would battle an army just to feel your back
pressed against his chest—will suffer.

Relationships in which both partners strive to express equal amounts of masculinity and femininity produce great friends. You will make cordial companions, but without opposing energies, your sexual encounters will rapidly cool to lukewarm.

These sugarless romances drive women to search for ways to sweeten the blandness. In their need for relief from the hollowing ache and their longing to be ravished by a masculine man in love, they search in vain for ways to fill the romantic void. Romance novels, comfort foods, shopping sprees, chocolate, and TV can only assuage a woman for so long. Sooner or later, the stifled energy of repressed needs balloons and manifests in a display of emotional outburst or harmful behavior. She'll become angry and act out, have an affair, divorce, fall into depression, become obese, drive herself into bankruptcy, or weep uncontrollably, unable to explain the source of her suffering. No matter how you try, the needs of the Divine Feminine will not be contained.

Most relationships today fall into one of three unfulfilling categories: (1) energetically neutral pair (boring, friends with benefits); (2) dominant female and submissive male (mother/adolescent boy, cougar/gigolo, smart woman/dummy man); and (3) overbearing masculine and weak feminine (boss man/secretary, chauvinist/bimbo, father/adolescent girl).

The most underrepresented, but fulfilling, relationship dynamic is between two people who express their masculine and feminine energies in a healthy and opposing manner. Though this book is written primarily for heterosexual feminine women, the substance of this message applies to feminine men, masculine women, and gay couples, too. Regardless of gender or sexual preference, opposing sexual polarity is the required dynamic for passionate romantic relationships. Polarity alone is not enough to build a healthy and lasting union, but it is a foundational component. A rightly chosen romance offers the healing support and companionship of a strong emotional bond as well as arousing, romantic passion when masculine and feminine sexual energies meet.

Before we go any further, I want to be clear that both men and women have feminine and masculine energies, and they must know how to access either when required. For example, a woman must be able to stand up for herself or protect her child, and she may tap masculine energies to quash a threat. All women should be able to protect, provide for, and honor themselves. However, in the context of romance, if you want to be adored, worshipped, and made to feel and be treated like the goddess you are, check your masculine energy at the threshold of your relationship's door and revel in the sensual, healing, and receptive powers of femininity.

Few women have experienced firsthand the enlivening and restorative treasures of a healthy relationship that includes a strong masculine-feminine polarity. The damsel, goddess, historical heroine, movie star, or romance novel protagonist whose experience you covet so deeply is a reflection of your feminine essence longing to be embraced by a committed man who boldly stands in his instinct to protect and preserve, and whose power is palpable as he opens the way for your deepest expressions of love to emerge. He frees you to lavish him with tenderness, feminine adoration, vulnerability, and uninhibited sexuality. For him, this is heaven on earth and life support. Your unfolding and bliss restores, rejuvenates, and inspires him. As you unfurl in the grace of femininity, his drive to protect and please you will intensify. Together, the masculine man and feminine woman mirror nature's most powerful forces. He is the power of an erupting volcano. She is the cooling sea. Together they create new lands.

My journey to my own femininity was as messy as it was unlikely. I grew up without a father and was imprinted with the belief that femininity is a synonym for weakness. As a teen, I brandished a tough-girl facade and became involved with several weak and abusive men, one of whom got me pregnant. Though I'd dreamed of living a life of joy and flowing femininity, when it came to real challenges, I didn't trust it.

In my early relationships, I chose men who were only interested in sex, or passive losers who wanted me to fight for their goals the way I fought for mine. When it came to sex, I couldn't understand what all the fuss was about. My experience of intercourse with men who were disconnected from their masculine power led me to rank sex lower than laundry on my list of "Things I'd Love to Do Tonight." After numerous backward attempts at love, I gave up. I stopped dating all together, preferring instead to study Cleopatra, Mata Hari, Veronica Franco, Marie Antoinette, and Aphrodite. Mesmerized by their powerful femininity, and longing to possess their mystique, I immersed myself in their stories.

The break from dating served me well. Studying powerfully feminine women, both real and mythological, cultivated within me a sense of a sublime energy, graceful power, and sisterhood with other women. Their pain, passion, and prayers shaped me. I learned about myself and how my thinking and choices had created my experiences. As I became aware of the healthy expression of romance, sex, and love, I began to notice it everywhere in the world. I could see the seeds of everything I loved in the women I admired alive in me. My true self, the nubile feminine goddess I'd worked so hard to hide and deny, was the most precious and powerful aspect of me. This moment of self-acceptance marked my renaissance.

Three years later, I fell deeply in love with a wonderfully masculine and loving man. He was driven, competitive, assertive, and ambitious in his career and outside dealings. With me, though, he was protective, supportive, encouraging, and absolutely adoring. As he stood in his manhood, my femininity blossomed. I became the woman I'd longed to be. Our relationship opened me to an appreciation of real and lasting sexual enjoyment and passion. Every sexual experience before him had been a mechanical act wholly devoid of heart and feelings. Though I'd been married before and had a child, this beautiful man claimed my true virginity and transformed me. The following excerpt, from my unpublished memoir, highlights the conscious choice I made to surrender to the goddess within:

My summer in France fed my feminine soul. Every painting, statue, garden, and ocean wave united me with the ethereal women I'd admired for so long. Each of them spoke to me whispering, "The goddess lives in you." On my wedding day, I wanted to embody these mystical beings, wielders of love, beauty, and creation. I wanted my fiancé to feel as though he were marrying Botticelli's Venus. I wanted to let the part of me I'd held hostage for so long go free in glorious expression. I surrendered to my deepest desires to be all woman—not a feminist, self-sufficient, powerhouse woman, but a radiant, vulnerable, blissful woman whose heart rests only in her lover's hand.

The following years were the most joyous and successful of both our lives. Embracing my femininity continued to enhance our romantic experiences, and a new level of emotional and sexual intimacy emerged. This bond served as a shelter, protecting us during the inevitable storms of life. For nearly a decade, we were deeply connected emotionally and romantically smitten. Our time together was painfully cut short when a devastating illness struck my beloved, but we lived more fully in 10 years than most couples do in a lifetime. With what I came to know about the level of union that is possible, I would have remained alone rather than settle for a lesser connection. Blessedly, I have gone on to another sublimely satisfying, loving, and secure relationship.

You deserve lasting and fulfilling, juicy-sweet love. Begin to allow the luminous power of femininity to fill your heart, and watch: a man called to honor you will claim his position on the throne beside you. Together, you'll lift one another up in joyous expression and growth.

We'll spend the rest of Part II exploring how to prepare for and attract a masculine man of character, and together create a deeply loving connection, satisfying romantic life, and joyful kingdom.

8

UNVEILING THE GODDESS

Beneath the shadowy veils of injuries past,
love cannot abide.
The Goddess must wake and cast off the veils
to beckon love's embrace.

Imagine the mess if you set out to bake your wedding cake using whatever you found in your pantry—a little salt, a jar of marmalade, cereal, and a dash of food coloring. Most people assemble their romantic relationships in much the same way, tossing in their unresolved fears, old wounds, bad habits, and self-loathing. They finish the mix with someone who they hope will "complete them." When the whole thing collapses, they lament that relationships don't work. Nonsense. Relationships created with the right ingredients do work. They're sticky sweet pleasures that support you in becoming your best self.

Juicy, fulfilling, lasting love doesn't come about by accident. Like a croquembouche—the exquisite and decadent French wedding cake you might choose to have at your wedding—the quality of the ingredients is as important as the technique.

When I met Debra, she was 38 years old, pregnant with her second child, and completely overwhelmed. She had an eight-month-old baby, a job, a mortgage, and a husband who'd decided he needed to "find himself." It seemed as though the self he sought was hiding somewhere on the Internet, because he spent endless hours online. Her husband, Greg, was a dud. He had no life purpose, no sense of responsibility, no connection to his daughter, and no problem letting his wife hold the house together while he chatted with virtual women.

When Debra expressed her disappointment and upset, Greg lashed out and called her names. During one particularly intense face-off, he accused her of being promiscuous, stating that he probably wasn't the father of either of their children. Debra called me, and between furious heaves and sobs she unloaded years of glossed-over anguish and simmering ire. She was livid at Greg, life, and God; they all had failed her. She had done everything right. She'd grown up, gone to college, started a career, and married a man she loved, and it all had blown up in her face.

I supported Debra as her marriage ended. We learned that the implosion of her life was not an unforeseeable fluke. All the information pointing to this outcome with Greg had been plainly visible all along, yet she couldn't see it in time to save her the trouble. Debra grew up with an absent father and a single mother who struggled to pay the bills. She had never known stability, security, or peace. A baseline state of cautious tension was familiar and normal to her.

As a teenager, Debra searched for security. Her greatest desire was to feel cared for and wanted. She went out with any man who was older, was employed, and showed even a whisper of interest in her. Invariably, her relationships failed. Men would cheat, disappear for weeks at a time, or blindside her and call the whole thing off. Every break-up added to Debra's feelings of instability and insecurity. In a valiant move toward stability, she shifted focus to getting an education, yet still held on to the hope it would make her more attractive to men.

At age 25, Debra was physically beautiful, pursuing a graduate degree, and still longing for someone to love her. Along came Greg—intelligent, funny, handsome, and eager to spend his life with her. With Debra's childhood wounds still raw, Greg's willingness to stick around seemed the answered prayer she'd been waiting for. Finally feeling validated and desired, she agreed to marry him immediately, ignoring every warning sign and red flag.

Whenever Greg was rude to female sales clerks, waitresses, or the lady next door, Debra overlooked it, chalking up his behavior to being in a hurry, being tired, or having a lot on his mind. Coming from a household led by a single mother, Debra had no objection to Greg's insistence that, as an equally capable gender, she should support the household. One night, Greg disappeared and missed a job interview the next morning. To Debra, it was a minor mistake, just like the many times before their marriage when Greg had stayed out all night, claiming he was too drunk to call her before bedtime. His behavior seemed normal because it was similar to the treatment her mom had received from various boyfriends.

Greg's own troubles ran deep. His father had physically abused him for 11 years while his alcoholic mother looked away, and when the rampages ended, she offered sloppy, drenching apologies. He couldn't respect her. Greg had never known what it was to really love or be loved.

Under the haze of co-dependent euphoria, Debra believed the wounds of the past would serve to bond them and bring them closer. Debra and Greg were broken and blinded. The relationship was doomed from the first hello, and it couldn't be any other way. Relationships do not fix people; they amplify what already exists.

I asked Debra not to date while we worked together, and take the time to heal and purify herself. She needed to understand the drivers that led her to make poor choices, and recognize that beneath her upsets and pain lives a woman worthy of every good thing life offers. She began to write about the difficult experiences of her childhood and the people who'd triggered her pain. It was difficult at times, but liberating. As she grasped an understanding of how she'd come to make her decisions, she gained clarity. She discovered that all of the limiting beliefs that had made her feel so small and insignificant weren't even hers. They had been formulated out of painful experiences and the words of people too wounded to know better. Debra had spent her lifetime thinking other people's thoughts—her mother's voice spoke the loudest. Hope rose over her heart as she realized she could let go of the past, abandon the lies she'd been taught about herself, and transcend the feelings of unworthiness she'd felt for so long. She could begin again.

Debra chose to pursue a path of forgiveness, self-discovery, and intensive self-care, making pleasure, peace, and her own well-being top priorities. She learned to love herself by doing things that demonstrated self-love and care, things she had withheld from herself in the past, hoping a man would come and give them to her. She began to write down the qualities she admired about herself and took time to celebrate her own successes. She learned to meditate, sculpt pottery, and do yoga. When she took her daughters to the park, she made friends with other mothers. Soon her life was full of new activities and self-appreciation. For the first time, it felt good to be alone.

Two years later, Debra met her match: Michael, a kind, attractive, generous man who makes her laugh from the depths of her belly. Not surprisingly, Michael had worked through his own personal collapse and made it to the other side. He says the best thing about his relationship with Debra is not that she gives him anything he can't give himself; it's simply that he adores her and her children, and life is better together. Debra feels the same.

The first step in creating the love you desire and deserve begins with healing, purifying, and loving yourself. The lover you attract will be your mirror, reflecting your best and worst. Any unhealed wounds, harmful beliefs, unworthiness, and heartaches you've collected will color every new relationship until you understand and resolve them in your mind and release them.

For a month or two, at least, take time away from dating and commit to exclusively dating yourself. Make this dating hiatus as much about your outer world as your inner being. Beautify your living space. Clean and organize it. Make the places you spend the most time feel joyful, nurturing, and loving. Flowers, pictures, music, art, beautiful fabrics, and inspirational books fill my most loved rooms. Shake the past from your body through meditation, yoga, exercise, drawing, painting, dancing, running on a beach, or taking a weekend trip to somewhere beautiful, alone.

Romance yourself. Learn to give yourself all the kindness, attention, time, and love you've wanted from others. Lavish yourself with praise and recognition for all of the good qualities you possess and the many wonderful things you've done. Too often, we withhold self-appreciation because we don't want to seem conceited or egotistical. Acknowledging the wonderful things about you is an important part of building self-esteem. It connects you to your power. Make it a daily practice to celebrate *you*.

Romancing yourself is powerful because when you genuinely hold yourself in high regard, it provides a foundation for you to be held in high esteem in every future relationship. The way you treat yourself slips through the ethers, training others how to treat you. Not only will you create a wonderful life, single or not, the woman who knows how to love herself will hook the healthiest gentleman in the room.

Reconnect with the child you used to be. Do some of the things she always wanted to do. Cater to her thoughts and feelings. Reassure her and let her know that she never has to be afraid, and that your grown-up self will protect, love, and support her, forever. Teach her how to love and be loved by loving her. Embrace every aspect of you, even your deepest and darkest places. Accept yourself just as you are. It's okay to be you.

While you're learning to love yourself, examine your childhood and relationship history. Consider hiring a great therapist, referred by someone you trust, to help you process and understand your past. Many people underestimate the impact that the beliefs and self-views they learned during their formative years have on every aspect of their lives as adults. That said, I am not advocating decades of stagnation while you rehash the past. You risk missing out on the present moment and preclude the possibility of a better future. The value of therapy is in exploring and unearthing the elements that drive and color your experience. Once identified, you can work to let go of the past and all that does not serve you. The ideal goal of a therapy plan is to reach a place where you are able turn your full attention toward creating the person and life you desire. You deserve to live as the happiest and healthiest version of you. This, in itself, is a worthwhile end, but here's a bonus: a happy woman is a sexy woman.

If you're spiritually inclined, use this time to commune with your Source. Acknowledge there are no accidents and accept that you're here on purpose. Dissolve the illusion that someone or something needs to choose you. You do not need a relationship or anything else to be complete. You are, and always have been, enough.

9

CONJURING ADONIS

The unclothed whisperings of the Goddess' soul
calls out across creation summoning
The One.

If you don't know what you're looking for in a man, you're not ready to meet him. Invariably, women argue with me about this. They say destiny will bring the right man to them or that it's exciting and fun to discover unexpected qualities in a new man. To which I reply, "Great, have at it." The next time you take a trip, eat at a restaurant, or change careers, let destiny handle it or tell the person helping you that you'll accept whatever they give you, and enjoy the excitement. No woman is willing to entrust the little decisions of her life to destiny, and most want what they want, not whatever shows up. Yet when it comes to romance, too often women check their common sense at the bedroom door.

If you've followed the guidance in the previous section ("Unveiling the Goddess") and taken a dating hiatus while purifying, healing, and rejuvenating yourself, you're clear about who you are. You've released baggage from past relationships and are in the throes of a love affair with yourself. If you haven't done this, please make the process easier and do so before continuing.

Once you've prepared the garden, the next step is to seed the ethers and conjure the man of your dreams. Before you imagine

Brad Pitt lying on a chaise longue wearing only a fig leaf and holding a rose and a black American Express card, remember that no one is perfect, including you and me. Don't get lost in a quagmire of superficiality. Focus on substance, the deal-making and deal-breaking qualities that matter to you the most. Avoid empty descriptions like: 5'11", 185 lbs, brown hair, green eyes, educated at the Sorbonne, and a seasoned polo player with a trust fund who is also generous and funny. He sounds like a delicious tart, doesn't he? But what if he's also a playboy with a nasty temper who insists his children go to boarding school, and he travels on business three weeks a month? The right description considers the realities of daily living and the qualities you need to create lasting love, happiness, and support as you pursue your goals.

If you plan on having children or you have them already, being a good mother starts here. The process of deciding what you're looking for in a man is an act of motherhood. The fate of your children, whom you will or already treasure more than your own heartbeat, will be heavily influenced by the quality of your man's presence. Not all men have temperaments or personalities suited to parenthood and home life. Don't assume that his desire for children means he'll be a good father. Wanting a soufflé doesn't make one a great chef. Even if you do believe he's ideal father material, there is more to consider. What religious or spiritual beliefs do you want your children to have, or not have? Is it important to you to stay home with them while they're young? How do want your children disciplined? One of the most painful experiences a woman can endure is watching someone educate or treat her children in a manner she opposes. Save yourself and your children by identifying what you want for them and choose a man who shares your desires.

Another hot topic is money, a leading cause of relationship strife. A woman often shies away from evaluating a man's relationship suitability in terms of finances because she's afraid to be seen as a gold digger. Let's end that now. To feel secure within a relationship, a deeply feminine woman requires an intensely masculine man. That means, though they are equal, they are different. She may work very hard in the home or in a career, but she needs a man who, among other things, strides out into the world and brings money home. Ignoring, denying, or criticizing this fundamental dynamic doesn't change it or negate its veracity. Just as many men need sex to feel loved, many women need protection and financial provision to feel cared for, safe, and happy. Own it, and save yourself from the sadness many women experience when they realize that they'd rather be alone than in marriages with men who, for no legitimate reason, fail to earn a sustainable living. Just because women can support a married household by themselves doesn't mean it makes them happy.

The amount a man earns, or will earn, is important in other ways, too. Women are biologically hardwired to nurture their young from the dependent state of newborn to early childhood, at least. If a woman wants to stay home with her child, she needs a man who supports that choice and can pay the bills. Consistent and adequate income is required to create security and stability within the home. A woman who takes time away from her career is likely to earn less than her counterparts who do not. Her partner must be willing and able to pick up the slack.

Do yourself a favor and insist that your Adonis have a life purpose and direction of his own, one he will not allow you to supplant. On its face, this may sound undesirable, but look deeper. A man with a definite life purpose is one you can count on to be strong, forward moving, and steadfast in the face of challenge. His life's mission is his kingdom, and it must exist apart from you. Ruling this kingdom well is his primary purpose. Don't be put off by the idea that his kingdom is more important than you. Your future is guaranteed to be miserable if he makes you his life's purpose. Imagine a king who abandons his throne to chase a princess; his kingdom will collapse. Few things are less attractive than a man with no direction or mission in life beyond his desire to love and dote on you. This sort of man is wallowing in his feminine energy and will force you into your masculine. It's the death knell for romance. Time and again, I've witnessed this joy-sucking dynamic unfold. At first, the woman, content to be in control, builds a life for the man, setting his goals for him and directing his actions. She assigns him a mission, monitors his progress, and continuously counsels and motivates him; she becomes his mother. When a woman adopts a mother role with her husband, eventually the sexual aspect of the relationship leaves her repulsed. When a man marries his mother, he'll soon need a girlfriend. I'm not endorsing his decision to step out on the marriage, but I understand the thought process. Kingdom-less men also tend to lack the substance and character required to honor commitments or uphold values against temptations. Be sure the man you invest in holds to his life purpose no matter what.

Of course, a suitable partner also must be committed to the relationship. Women, by nature, are in a perpetual state of transition and emotional flux. Our bodies generate cyclical hormones that influence our moods and emotions, even after the childbearing years are over. On top of this, we are intuitive and sensual energetic beings who easily absorb the emotions and feeling tones of others.

There is one predictable aspect of the female mind: change. This doesn't mean we're crazy. It means that we can be counted on to have strong, temporary feelings. We may bring the sadness of a friend home with us. Sometimes hormonal shifts shorten our patience, and we become snappy or sullen. Some days, seeing one more sock, dirty dish, sporting event, or (insert your barely tolerated peeve here) sends you over the edge. I've met several women who at certain points in the month come to despise their normally treasured career or marriage, and during those times they genuinely believe their feelings are true. This is an extreme example, but it helps illustrate the idea. The absolute last thing a woman feeling the pull of her emotions needs is a man who freaks out and becomes an emotional wreck himself.

As he expresses through his feminine, she'll be forced to compensate with her masculine characteristics or risk the two of them spinning out together. It takes a strong masculine man to hold a relationship steady and keep it on track through the storms.

To sum up, be sure that when you conjure the perfect Adonis, you include providing income, a strong work ethic, an independent life mission, and a steadfast commitment to the relationship on your "must haves" list. Acknowledge and accept your needs, and hold out for them. It's as greedy and selfish as filling a canteen with water for a trek across the Sahara.

If more women were honest about their needs and refrained from marrying and having children in situations that failed to meet those needs, divorce rates would be lower and we would save our children and ourselves much heartache. As more women hold out for men who will protect, provide for, and lead their families, men will rise to the expectation and make it a priority. This creates a win for all: the children will have stability and both men and women will be happier.

Just as important as knowing what you want is knowing what you *don't* want. These are the deal-breakers, the biggies that you just can't or won't tolerate. To save you from going grey while you kiss a thousand frogs in search of a prince, you must know in advance what you refuse to accept in a man. Make your list and stick to it. Start with these red flags: drug use, alcoholism, abandonment of a child, perpetual unemployment, hostility, cruelty, highly possessive/jealous nature, stingy, racist, critical, womanizing, lacking follow-though, and dishonesty. Once you've completed your list of deal-breakers, make an unbreakable vow that if any of these traits show up, the romance is over. Indulge no second chances or mental machinations about how you might be the one to change him. You aren't.

Here's a description of an ideal mate and deal-breakers written by my client and friend, Cara. She stumbled across her prince charming at a horse show six months after she wrote it. She recognized her man immediately, because she already knew exactly who he was.

CARA'S ADONIS

The man I will spend my life with is kind, trustworthy, and stable. He returns calls, does what he says he will do, and has good relationships with his family and friends. He is completely single and emotionally, physically, and legally available. He wants children—both mine and the ones we'll have together. We have deep conversations, and he expresses his feelings easily. In disagreements, he remains respectful. He is easy to be around and doesn't criticize others. He makes me laugh, and he's secure in himself. He values our relationship and continuously courts me. When he puts his arms around me, I melt. We have a rich sex life. He has a career that he enjoys and a strong work ethic. He is financially responsible, takes care of his health, and practices good hygiene. He supports me in my desire to stay home with the children. We are spiritual and enjoy raising our children to be, too. He encourages me to pursue my dream of owning an art gallery. My deal-breakers are: verbal or physical abuse, lying, infidelity, attempting to dominate me (or others), physical aggression toward anyone, unpredictable moodiness, drugs, alcoholism, and smoking.

When a woman knows what she desires in a man, she can recognize men who aren't a good fit long before any attachment forms, saving both parties time and hurt feelings. She is also able to recognize dream guy potential in a man she might have overlooked in the past.

10
ATTRACTING LOVE

For the woman connected to her feminine wisdom,
attracting love is as natural as inhaling.
She is born knowing how.

To attract love, fall in love with life. The whole of life turns its gaze on a being living in love. Creation smiles at the discovery of its own magnificence. Men are no different; they are irresistibly drawn to the energy of a woman consumed by love and grace. Cultivate this fulfilling state by noticing and appreciating the unbounded beauty and exquisite majesty of the world around you. There is much to adore: looking into the eyes of a woman who saw this world before you were born, the miracle of a baby's plump thigh, the mighty energy that sends trees stretching toward the sky, and the pulse in your wrist; all are calls to love. You can spend a lifetime crying out for love, or realize you are sitting in its palm.

Another man magnet is real sex appeal, and it's not what you might think. The sexiest woman in the world is happy with herself. She feels whole and complete, with or without a man. She doesn't exude an ounce of neediness. She has no inclination to connive to snag a man, seduce someone else's, or pretend she doesn't want one. She's bubbling with life, actively pursuing interests that matter to her, and at peace with herself. She's done the work to become the counterpart to her divine match, and she trusts that all things happen in the right time. For her, there is no question of whether her match will appear, only when, and she's patient, knowing she cannot rush the sunrise.

Women once knew and trusted their innate feminine wisdom. Throughout history, this divine knowing has been repressed and denied by a ruling patriarchy. Today, women have the freedom to follow their knowing, but they face a new adversary: the entertainment and advertising industries. When the feminine mind accepts the backward thinking promulgated by the media, she loses confidence and trust in her supreme wisdom. She lives from the premise that something is wrong with her if she doesn't have a man in her life.

In addition, the media's distorted view of what men want—combined with the countless number of myths circulating in women's magazines and trash TV—covers up the truth about male desires. According to popular culture, men are attracted to thin, busty, overly made-up sex kittens. Nothing could be further from the truth. Granted, there are men who buy into this contrived image, but women needn't pay them an ounce of attention because they lack the qualities that a woman of substance requires. (See "Conjuring Adonis.")

Another force that can undermine a woman's feminine knowing is other women. A woman's definition of beauty and a man's are vastly different. Women are far more critical. Many women believe the advertisers, who tell her the newest shoes, hairdo, and spray tan will make her more beautiful than other women. They spend small fortunes on fashion, cosmetics, and jewelry to impress other women. Instead of working to become sexy (genuinely happy with themselves) these lost women invariably find themselves staring into their mirrors obsessing over "imperfections."

To men, this noise is an unattractive distraction from the exquisite symphony of qualities they value. Women who are slaves to fashion, cosmetics, and outward appearance place an obstacle between themselves and men. To overcome it, a woman must compensate with high doses of what healthy men really want: a genuine, friendly, fun, and self-loving woman. Ladies, do yourselves a favor, return to you. It's the sexiest thing you can do.

I asked a number of men living in the Western world to describe what they find most attractive in a woman. I expected to receive a few scant responses. I grossly miscalculated. Within moments of my request, I received posts and e-mails from men offering detailed descriptions of what they found most beautiful in a woman.

Contrary to the emotionally blunted image portrayed in the media, men are deeply aware of their feelings and need for intimacy. They may not sit like ladies at tea, tearing up as they share their desire for real love, but it's there, and it burns like an inferno. With all confidence, I am thrilled to report that men of all ages, races, and places are brimming with real love to give. They desire so much more than a sexual playmate. If you've lost your faith in men, or just want some reassurance, here's a small sample of the descriptions I received from men about what they find attractive:

> "I don't have a type. What I like is a lady who feels good in her skin. She doesn't have to wear a lot of makeup or whatever. She has to take care of herself, though. A woman who takes good care of herself will take good care of me, too. It's also important that she's happy most of the time and a nice person."

> "Intelligence, eyes, and spunk."

"A sense of self, which leads to confidence. A woman who understands her worth and doesn't stand for those who don't respect it. A willingness to care actively for others, and an eagerness to embrace her physical beauty."

"An open mind, a caring heart, a feminine grace, an implicit innocence, a confident beauty (not a shallow, made-up, pretty one, though pretty is not being ruled out here), a trusting nature, a reciprocating mirror of love."

"Open, honest, transparent, with nothing to hide, caring of herself and mindful of others."

"Femininity, as in making the man feel masculine by seeking his protection. Strong women who are not afraid to show vulnerability. Femininity exists to balance masculinity, and masculinity to balance femininity."

"Beauty attracts as much as it gives. Women who attract have attributes like honesty, integrity, and faith; and by their sheer inner core magnetism, they reflect it back by a smile, a touch, or an act of giving. They say, 'Beauty is in the eye of the beholder,' but beauty is *not* only in the eye of the beholder; it's in the heart and soul of a woman."

"The physical aspects of the fairer sex are a consideration, but the one that least concerns me! I prefer substance to overt sexuality! But, then again, the *right substance* can be, and *is*, quite *sexually* enticing!"

"One: A woman who's comfortable in herself. A sense of self-possession, despite any 'flaws' she thinks she might have.

"Two: Radiant kindness. Anyone can be 'tough,' but, to my mind, true strength lives in kindness.

"Three: A woman who finds me as beautiful as I find her. If a woman can genuinely treat a man as if he has earned her complete and utter attention to the exclusion of just about everyone else . . . that he's one of the top priorities in her life (basically, runner-up to her spiritual beliefs and, of course, herself) . . . she's an unprecedentedly magical being!

"Four: Energetically, it's about energy that declares person-hood, then womanhood, then sex. It's energy that moves and says, 'Watch me. Look at who I am and what I'm capable of.' But it's conveyed effortlessly, as a part of her, not something she has to make happen.

"Five: Physically, I'm fond of very hourglass bodies . . . wide shoulders/hips particularly, and good skin, but I put this last because it's the least consideration. Everything else trumps it."

Notice how large a role feminine confidence plays in attraction. Not to be confused with masculine assertiveness, feminine confidence is the easy comfort of a woman connected to her essence and secure in her mind and body. She exudes a sense of "This is who I am, and I'm comfortable with it" that magnetizes men. They crave women who enjoy being themselves, not those who strive to mimic the unreal images on TV.

One final, but immensely important, aspect of attracting love is being open and receptive to attention from gentlemen. Though it is innately feminine to receive, this ability is sometimes muddled by fear, discomfort, or a mistaken belief that being receptive to attention from men is akin to being easy or loose. Being open and receptive to connecting with a well-behaved human being is universally appropriate behavior and, at this point in the courting process, it will not be construed as being an easy lay.

Consider the plight of a man seeking a woman to share his life. He must (1) ensure that his personal and professional affairs are in order (men already know that a woman worth having has standards and needs); (2) set out to meet a woman who sparks his curiosity and interest; (3) do his best to determine whether she's available and open to being approached; (4) muster up the courage to engage her; and then (5) risk rejection by asking her on a date. If he miscalculates and discovers she's married, in love with someone else, or she flat out rebuffs him, he has to start all over again. Imagine repeating this process countless times. It's challenging and, as a woman, it sounds excruciating. There is nothing I'd like to do less. Help men find their match by being receptive, kind, and clear. In the process, you'll discover your match.

11

YOU: THE GODDESS INCARNATE

A Goddess's only unforgiveable sin is
rejecting her beauty, outside and within.

Right now, you already have all of the raw material to be a true beauty. You don't need to buy anything. If you're feeling insecure, make your care and happiness a priority. Develop your interests and build friendships with women who carry themselves with the kind of feminine confidence you admire (you admire it because it's alive in you). Nurture yourself, be kind, and set time aside to do things that fulfill you. Worship the creation that you are, and seek out everything magnificent around you. In your happiness lies the elixir of radiant beauty.

No discussion about magnetizing men would be complete without acknowledging and addressing their nature and hard-wired attraction to physical beauty. Men are visual creatures, and most women know this. What you may not know is that unlike you, he doesn't obsess over your weight. He's not bothered by a few extra pounds; more often he loves them. If you are significantly overweight, what men think is far less important than the reasons you aren't valuing yourself enough to take care of your health. (See "Unveiling the Goddess.") Men of character aren't wishing you'd get plastic surgery, wear hair extensions, or strut around in six-inch stilettos. The vast majority of desirable men want you to take good care of your health and hygiene, and present yourself in a flattering way by dressing in a manner that makes you feel beautiful inside. Caring for yourself sends a message to the world that you also care about your man and your family. It tells your man that you enjoy looking good for him. It makes him feel proud, privileged, and valued.

When I pressed men to list the physical attributes they crave, their answers varied widely. Some men love wide shoulders and hips; others love full breasts and small behinds; and many specifically prefer the opposite (small breasts and large behinds). Many men said "it" was all in the eyes and/or smile. The basic fact is that there are men out there who crave your specific body type. In dating and life, you can never please everyone, so don't try. Please yourself, and those who are similarly pleased will find you.

I'd be remiss not to mention two physical characteristics that the overwhelming majority of men agreed on: soft, smooth skin and longer blonde, auburn, brown, or black hair. As always, there are exceptions, and some women look best rockin' a pixie cut. Most grown men do not want to date "Rainbow Brite," so no fuchsia, blue, or green hair, please.

In summary, what the majority of men want most is a woman who is clean, wearing light makeup, and dressed in an appropriate way that flatters her body and shows she cares about herself and feels beautiful. So ditch the face frosting; the ring in your nose; the stained, nipple-hugging tank; flannel anything; and the greasy updo. Instead, wash and polish your body to a state of sublime softness; use a light dusting of mineral makeup; wear clean, attractive clothes that fit; and wash your hair into a luxurious cascade. Look good. Feel good. Smell good. Voila! You're a hottie!

12

DATE LIKE A VENETIAN

Patient restraint of passion and plans
places the heart, hearth, and home of a
King in her hands.

Most writings on dating tell a woman how to look and what to say in order to get a date. This is a miserable short sale of a woman's worth. The rules are simple: be yourself, honor your life's desires, enjoy the process, and check your masculinity (but not your common sense) at the door. Right now, you are someone's dream girl and goddess. Know it.

A line from one of my favorite movies about feminine power, *Dangerous Beauty*, expresses the desires of a masculine man best: "In order to choose your lovers wisely, you need to understand men. No matter their shape or size, position or wealth, they all dream of the temptress—the irresistible, unapproachable Venus who quickly turns pliable maiden when they've had a hard day."[1] Men everywhere are thirsting for Venus.

Knowing when to shape-shift among temptress, Venus, and maiden is a vital skill. On first contact, embody the maiden: be friendly, approachable, and receptive. When a potential suitor presents himself, smile, make eye contact, and be open to meeting a fellow human. Meanwhile, keep your Adonis requirements silently in mind. If you sense this man isn't right for you, kindly tell him.

If you're interested in getting to know him better, communicate it by looking into his eyes frequently, without staring. Smile and face him with the front of your body, keeping your arms uncrossed. Let the mystery of not knowing whether he is your Adonis or a dead end hold your emotions and personal information in reserve. You must give him some walls to climb later. Let him experience your beauty, inner light, and feminine grace while things are new—this is *being* Venus. Never grill a new acquaintance about his life plans, income, past relationships, religion, family, or politics on your first several dates. It's off-putting and masculine. Follow your intuition, relax, and let him court you. If you sense he may have the qualities that are important to you, wait for him to ask to see you again and accept graciously. Allow him to make all of the arrangements and handle communications between you. Many women feel it's appropriate to help out by asking for a date or phone number, or planning the date's activities. Unless you want to be the laboring oar in your relationship, don't do it. A man who is unwilling to work to be with you now is certain to do no work later in the relationship. Let him walk away with nothing, and forget all about him. Hold out for a man who courts, leads, and pursues you.

These first interactions set the tone for the whole relationship and must follow a dynamic that allows you to be grounded in your feminine energy, and he in his masculine. Using your masculine traits in romance will amplify his feminine aspects or cause friction, and neither outcome will lead to happiness. Learn to leave your masculine energy at the door of your dating life. Create the setting for the romance you desire. Remember, it's hard for a man to sweep you off your feet if he's wearing a dress and heels.

When you let your date lead, you get to sit back and experience his personality, style, tastes, and financial habits. Look for qualities that match the description of your Adonis. Meanwhile, be mindful of your inner state. Watch your emotions. If you begin to feel desire and warmth, be sure to balance it against the reality of what you're looking for in a man. Though it may feel like you're taking the fun out of the party, be alert for any qualities and behaviors that might upset you in a relationship as they emerge. If he doesn't call when he says he will now, just wait. It will only get worse once he's comfortable.

Resist any temptation to alter your description of your Adonis to suit the man you're dating, and never reconsider a deal-breaker. You will not change him, so don't ever believe you can. Please listen. Putting an end to dating someone you're attracted to, but who is not a good fit, is far superior to intertwining bodies, emotions, finances, families, and children, and being tormented later.

Suppose you discover a man who just may be your Adonis. He's fabulous, hitting all of your targets, and free of any deal-breakers. You've dated a few times and things couldn't be any more blissful. Staring into his eyes, you see a lifetime of laughter, friendship, and sex more delicious than sticky toffee pudding. You enjoy another perfect evening together, he holds you close, and together you silently agree that tonight is the night you stamp his heart with your mark and make love to him. Stop. Before you allow him the blessing of your feminine form, consider three important points: (1) Men value the rare find; (2) You are biologically hardwired to release hormones that will unilaterally bind you to whomever you have sex with; and (3) Premature sex undermines the likelihood of a man falling in love with you.

Men are hardwired to seek and acquire precious and rare treasure. Though this most obviously applies to jewels, money, and rare objets d'art, a man will go to great lengths to woo a woman he perceives to be a rare find. I am continuously baffled by women who throw this truism off the nearest barstool and jump into bed with a man they just met on Friday, swear they're in love on Saturday, and spend the week dreaming of a lifetime together—only to find themselves sitting at home alone the following Thursday, wondering why "Mr. Wonderful" hasn't called. He isn't busy, and he hasn't lost her phone number. He enjoyed the romp and moved on.

Much of society has rebelled against and done away with religious, social, and gender-biased admonitions against premarital and promiscuous sex. Since the 1960s, there has been a backlash against prohibitions or limitations on sex free of commitment. The "free love" ideal rebelled against the old-guard mores, calling them oppressive and driven by the desire to control people, namely women. Though the shame and ostracizing of women who engaged in premarital sex was reprehensible and deserves no return to power, refraining from casual sex is a wise choice. This is not due to moral or religious righteousness; it's simply feminine smarts and self-love.

Offering sex before commitment dramatically diminishes the likelihood of a man wanting a long-term, monogamous relationship with you. Men are driven to desire a woman they feel is special, a treasure. Engaging in sex before mutually agreeing to a monogamous relationship is no more of a special event than mating farm animals. To you, it may feel like a gesture of love and heartfelt bonding. To him, it sends a message: "This isn't a big deal to me; I do this with all the men I really like." Many men will partake and enjoy casual sexual relationships, but when it comes time to picking a life partner, the "easy mark" won't be in the running. Men will search for a woman who refuses to engage in such an important behavior without a serious relationship. They'll go for the rare find.

If being on the same level as livestock in heat isn't enough to end a woman's freewheeling sex days forever, consider the power of the "love hormone," oxytocin. Responsible for creating emotional attachment between a mother and her newborn baby, this hormone induces feelings of well-being; decreases fear, anxiety, and inhibition; and increases feelings of trust and calm. In addition to childbirth, research indicates that sexual activity and affection cause female oxytocin levels to rise, too, encouraging us to develop an emotional attachment to the person we're having sex with.[2] The oxytocin effect lingers. Even if our rational brain understands that he's the wrong guy, oxytocin will cause us to have warm fuzzy feelings of connection and desire for him. This explains why so many women return to and pine after men they don't really respect or like as people. I've talked to several women who liken the experience to a bout of temporary insanity. They weren't insane; they were experiencing the biochemical results of engaging in sexual intimacy with an unsuitable partner.

Beyond biochemical responses and the message your sexual behavior sends to a man, be keenly aware of the energetic shifts caused by sex. For me, the number one reason I avoid casual sex is that I am unwilling to let a man inside the temple of my spirit before we share mutual love, respect, and admiration. Our emotions, energy, and well-being are inextricably bound to sex. Orgasm is both a physical and a spiritual experience. It opens up our energy centers, and we become vulnerable, both in the energy we exude and the energy we receive. There is no such thing as spiritual contraception. Many liken orgasm to the bliss of enlightenment. In this moment of openness, you take on your partner's energies, be they uplifting, healing, wounded, or toxic. His energy mingles with yours and becomes part of you.

All manner of outcomes, from wondrous to soul-ripping, are possible. If your partner is in an energetic state of consumption, feeding off of other people's energy, he can drain you. Energy vampires often hang on—feeding on your spiritual and physical energy, and sucking you dry—until you are thoroughly depleted. The risks are grave.

Everything you create, feel, think, and do depends upon the quality and tone of your energy. It's just plain smart to protect and support it. The man you allow inside the temple of your spirit will biologically and energetically become a part of you.

When mutual love, respect, and commitment are absent, there is a great threat of energetic harm, and the more feminine your essence, the more deeply you'll feel it.

Plainly put, casual sex is an oxymoron for women.

The role of managing the sexual energy in a new relationship belongs to you. When you grasp your power to govern the flow of sexual energies, you become an alchemist able to transmute raw, animalistic drives into sublime love.

Male sexual attraction begins in the loins and, if properly contained and channeled, it flows upward toward his heart and mind. When you handle your sexual power rightly, it simmers and folds in upon itself, intensifying, and simultaneously saturating your lover's heart. Once your energy completely envelops his heart, he will no longer simply lust after you like a hound in a butcher's shop. In addition to wanting to ravish you sexually, he'll desire you with every aspect of his being.

A wise woman knows that to protect her heart and sustain a man's love, she must temper her passions and refrain from sex until his mind, loins, and heart synchronize. If a man's heart fails to catch up with his loins, there is no romance to be had. She must end the relationship and move on.

No woman can make a man love her through sex or intellect. She may titillate him or induce a chemical dependence on the pleasures of her form, or she may interest him in lively conversation, but she will not sway his heart. Capturing his mind and loins won't be enough. He will grant his loyalties to the woman who captures his heart.

A man can spend an indefinite amount of time in a relationship built on mind and loins alone. He can remain engaged and withhold his heart. Women cannot. Even if we think we can, we can't. Never allow your desire for a man to cause you to settle for less than his whole heart. If he does not offer it, face whatever pain you must and remove yourself from the relationship. The agony will only be worse if you wait. You deserve all of him: mind, heart, and loins. If you discover that you've reached a dead end, leave the relationship and make way for the love you really want.

NOTES

1. Quote used with the gracious permission of Jeannine Dominy, writer of the screenplay, *Dangerous Beauty*, Warner Bros. 1998.

2. See Cindy M. Meston and Davis M. Buss's *Why Women Have Sex: Understanding Sexual Motivations—From Adventure to Revenge (And Everything In Between)* (New York: Times Books, 2009) pp. 69-71.

13

HOW TO LOVE A MAN

Inside every man is a hero, a king, a passionate lover,
an adoring husband, and a loving father.
Left to himself, one or two aspects may emerge in the world,
but the masterful love of a woman frees them all.

Before we delve into the minds of men and what they require
to feel loved and satisfied, I'd like to clarify that the information
in this section applies to the majority of men, particularly masculine men. There are exceptions to every rule, and not all men
are masculine. Please don't take my statements too literally or
to nonsensical extremes. When I write, "Give your man control
or power," it means give it to him so long as it does not disturb
or harm you or someone else. For example, handing decision-
making power over to your husband is a fabulous way to amplify
his sense that you trust and respect him. However, if the question
at hand is whether to buy a house, have plastic surgery on your
body, or adopt a child, allowing him to decide on your behalf is
ridiculous. N'est-ce pas?

Next, please understand that certain facts about men may
upset you if you take them personally. Understand that men have
different compositions, outlooks, and drives. You must not take
his innate presets as evidence of his disrespect for womankind or

you. You can, however, expect him to control his behavior or do without you.

Finally, not all men are good men, and you cannot change them. This admonition is particularly poignant for me because when I was a teen, I had a boyfriend who lied and cheated regularly. Determined to end his philandering, I purchased a book titled something like, *How to Keep Your Man Monogamous*. The book detailed how to make a man feel wanted, satisfied, and fulfilled so he wouldn't dream of going anywhere else for love. While much of the book's content was valuable in the context of two people who love each other and value monogamy, in my situation, it was tantamount to frosting a pile of manure and calling it a cake. The same goes here. This chapter is for women who love, or intend to love, a man with integrity, values, and a desire for monogamy.

14

RETURN HIM
TO THE THRONE

"Finally," the Queen rejoiced, "I need not work alone.
The warring is over; the King returns to his throne."

A first and vitally important step in loving a man is to return him to his throne. Distorted feminism in the form of masculine "independent" women, and the media's negative representation of men, have come together to throw men off the throne and under a bus.

Modern women routinely gab about their incapable husbands, who couldn't manage their lives without them. They see men as incompetent and no longer trust them to solve problems or make decisions. Fathers are no longer viewed as necessary participants in child-rearing. More and more children are raised in households headed by women and grow up with no direct experience of a man in a healthy, positive leadership role.

When a man opens the door for a woman, he risks being chastised. Good men everywhere report feeling confused, frustrated, and wary of offending women with traditional gentlemanly manners. In every way, men in Western society have been diminished, and the worst of male behavior receives the lion's share of attention.

This is certainly true in the media, which portrays men as womanizers, slobs, emasculated toddlers in grown bodies, and babbling morons who can't function without a woman to tell them what to do. Challenge yourself to identify 10 decent, respectable, competent, and masculine men in current television programming. You won't find them because they aren't there.

Sometimes, in the simple effort to get things done right the first time, women second-guess, challenge, or just take over a man's decisions. When a man stops using his leadership abilities, like the muscles in a body, they atrophy. The more responsibility and accountability women take from men, the less confident and competent men become. In romantic relationships, interfering with or eliminating a man's domain of handling problems and making decisions sends the clear message: "I don't trust or respect you." Women may not consider this message all that terrible, until they understand its equivalent. Telling a man "I don't respect or trust you," has the same impact on him that saying "I don't love or want you," would have on you.

One tragic consequence of ousting men from the throne is that men have changed to meet our lowered expectations. They no longer feel the same impetus to "do the right thing," to provide for a family or handle their commitments with honor. We women then complain that there are "no good men out there" and use our conclusion as an excuse to endure and even fight to keep deceitful, free-loading, inappropriate, offensive, and abusive men. Believing there's nothing better out there, we race each other to the bottom.

Men will do what they have to do to attain what they want. No less. If we require nothing of them, we can expect nothing. If we refuse to engage in sex and relationships with men who insist on remaining perpetual children, who harm or betray other women, who lie, cheat, or leave, they quickly realize that to satisfy their needs they must become, and remain, better men. Our power and duty as women, mothers, and sisters is to raise the bar and invite men back to their rightful place as leaders, lovers, and heroes.

Return your man to the throne by allowing him to fix things, solve problems, figure things out, and make decisions without your involvement. He doesn't need you to tell him how to fold the grocery bags, what route to take in traffic, how to handle a dispute with a sales clerk, or what to say to the children. When you feel yourself jumping up and down inside, eager to tell him how to do something "right," zip it and turn your attention to something you're interested in: your work, a project, a daydream, something you'd like to create.

Ask for his help. Ask his advice. Let him come to your rescue every now and then. Enjoy the easy feeling and freedom of carrying less of the burden and having a man who has your back, a man you can trust. He needs you to need him. You cannot comfortably sit on both thrones. It's okay to let go.

15

YOUR WORD IS YOUR WAND

The power to exalt or wound a man
rests in her tongue, not her hands.

Women's words are powerful incantations, capable of causing or preventing conflict, building or devastating a man's confidence, and drawing out his misery or magnificence. Perhaps due to men's unwillingness to express or show emotional hurt, most women underestimate the exquisite sensitivity of men, all men, regardless of their level of masculinity. Beneath their seemingly unperturbed exterior lies tenderness equal to, if not greater than, a woman's. Unfortunately for men, they aren't comfortable reaching out to friends and support groups to share their hurt and receive healing feedback. They ache alone.

A woman often lacks any appreciation of the gut-twisting effects her thoughtless words have on her man. In a rush to get the day moving, she may criticize his choices, complain about perceived shortcomings, and boss him around. Though she likely wouldn't stand for a man who treated her in the same way, she doesn't realize that each time she lobs a negative remark at him, it creates a micro-tear in his heart. Over time, deep sadness, resentment, and despair create a smoldering pit of desire to be free, to feel loved and enlivened again. This desire may manifest in an affair. While it does not justify such a betrayal, it does, however help to reveal his motivation. Many men will simply suffer in silence. They won't make the self-preserving decision to get out of an emotionally castrating relationship. They remain in the toxic environment as it kills them slowly.

You can heal and empower your man, both in his life at home and in the world, simply by choosing words and behaviors that summon the best in him. If you've developed a pattern of micromanaging your man, you will have to use self-discipline to extend your trust first and allow his trustworthy behavior to follow. Affirm and appreciate him by acknowledging that you respect, admire, and trust him. Tell him you're proud of him. Let him know that he's the *one* for you. Trust in his judgment, decisions, and abilities. Even in—especially in—tough times, economic downturns, crises, and difficulties, honor his heart and build his confidence. A man fortified by the immunizing love of a woman can carry two Earths on his shoulders.

Never cut him down or humiliate him. These behaviors are so caustic to the tender masculine heart that they cannot be ignored or tolerated.

Maria and Sid were married for nearly 20 years. Sid spent a major part of the first 15 years away on business trips, while Maria stayed home with the children. Their marriage was generally peaceful, aside from pressures arising out of his frequent travels. Sid explains that once he sold his business and no longer had a reason to be away from home, he realized that he'd never survive life with Maria.

"At home, I felt like a loser," he said. "Maria always told me what I was doing wrong and how I should be better. She blamed me for her unhappiness. She said the kids and I robbed her of the life she could have had. I worked for 15 years, built a business on my back, and gave everything I had to her and our kids. She never noticed. She just kept complaining. She always compared me to other husbands and said she wanted what other women had; it used to kill me. When we went out with other couples, she made jokes about how dumb or lazy I was and how I'd be lost without her. One day, I realized that I was lost with her, too, so when our youngest turned 18, I left. Now she says she loves me and I'm the best man in the world, but for me, it's over. I'm much happier now."

Never mock or make deprecating jokes about your man. In private, it's emasculating and painful; in public, it's abuse. If you tend toward snarky moods, remind yourself that you will never hurt your man without hurting yourself. Build him up instead. Let everyone who meets you experience the reverence you feel for him. Know that to compare a man to another man is a venomous act. Even comparisons you think are harmless can cause grave harm to his sense of self-efficacy and worth. For example, when you say, "Jane and John seem so happy and in love," unless you immediately follow it up with "like us," your man hears, "I wish I had a man like that." In feminine speak, it's like your lover said, "I'd love to take Jane to a romantic dinner and make love to her tonight." To women this example may seem extreme, but to men it's dead-on.

A fatal mistake many women make in loving a man is to take him for granted or assume that he can't make it without them; he can. It may not be what he wants, but he can only handle so much emotional mistreatment or emasculation before he is faced with the choice between his very essence and you. If he chooses you, you'll burn forever in the flames of his resentment.

You have the power to harness the totality of the majestic masculine powers with your affirming words. Use your gifts wisely.

16

HE WANTS TO
BE YOUR HERO

Creating a hero is a simple art,
requiring only a need, his solution,
and your appreciative heart.

A man derives a deep sense of fulfillment and value when he is a hero in your eyes. He feels proud, powerful, needed, and successful in his manhood. This doesn't mean men desire damsels in distress, but if your car is stuck in the snow and he offers to come over and dig you out, let him. He will get more out of this act of service than you. It's his way of showing you that he loves you. When he sees you feeling ecstatic and appreciating his efforts, he will feel like a powerful and successful man.

One of the most significant ways men feel like a heroes is by providing for and supporting their household. Even if it's not expressed or demonstrated, the overwhelming majority of men feel a deep desire and a duty to provide. The drive to contribute material support is so strong that even if his wife earns enough to maintain the home and family, he will still want to provide.

Consequently, if he struggles or fails to meet the financial needs of the home, it cuts deeply into his sense of self-worth. In these times of struggle, though she may feel afraid, a woman must stand steadfast with her man and communicate her belief that he'll solve the problem. She may choose to take on work, cut expenses, and make other adjustments, but she must present these actions as smart moves taken to help get them through to the other side. If she expresses disappointment or a lack of confidence in him, she'll shred his already hemorrhaging heart and damaged self-esteem.

17

SEX: THE MASCULINE MAN'S LOVE LANGUAGE

Abandon inhibitions to keep the heart of your man;
give him raw passion like no other can.

Sex is central to any discussion about loving a man. Before we go any further, let's get something straight: the sex I'm talking about here is between two people who love each other and are in a monogamous relationship. There are always a few women who want put the motor on the front of the boat and use sex to create love. It doesn't work. It will never work. Love must come first, and jumping in the sack before love develops makes it far less likely that love will occur.

Men love sex. I'm not telling you anything new with that one. They'll take as much as you can give and want a whole lot more, but it might surprise you to know that it's not just the sex act they need. To feel emotionally loved, your man needs you to want to have sex with him and enjoy it, too. They want to literally see you, feel you, and hear you honestly enjoying yourself.

Men express and experience intimacy differently than women. Imagine going through life unable to hear your man's words of appreciation or love. Every time he said, "I love you" or "you're beautiful," all you were able to hear was static noise. Now imagine that he has some very special water, and whenever you drink it the static stops and you can hear his words of love clearly. You'd probably want to drink a lot of this water, and if you couldn't have it very often, you'd feel grumpy.

Now imagine knowing that your man has a vault full of this wonderful water and, if he wanted to, he could give you a whole bottle every day. That's how a man feels about sex and you. To him, you have the power to shower him with love, but sometimes (and according to many men, often) you choose to withhold it. He needs sex to feel loved.

Women, on the other hand, don't require a lot of sex to feel loved. We may like it, but we need other things more. We need protection, adoration, attention, interest, trust, and understanding before we feel the expansive warmth of love overflow our hearts and fill our bodies. On top of this, a woman's desire and willingness to have sex can easily be stymied by a variety of things. Exhaustion, worry, hormones, children, family, and changes in women's bodies can snuff out a woman's libido in an instant.

There is no perfect solution to out-of-sync sexuality, but both men and women can get a lot more of what they need to feel loved by communicating openly and choosing to work together to satisfy one another. Women must be willing to have sometimes blush-inducing conversations and tell men exactly what makes them happy in bed. We also need to ask for help with responsibilities that exhaust us, so we'll have the energy to make love. We may choose to have a quickie or occasionally agree to an unwanted romp to make our man happy. This is perfectly fine, so long as it comes from a motivation of love. Once the interaction gets started, desire may kick in anyway. At no time should you begrudgingly give in to sex. This is a soul-ripping act that divides you against yourself.

One of the most effective ways to hurt a man is to manipulate him with your sexuality. Conditioning sex on anything is tantamount to him conditioning his love on sex with you. If your man told you that he'd love you if you agreed to clean out the garage, wash the dog, or change a diaper, but he wouldn't love you if you didn't do these things, you'd kick him to the curb, I hope. Using sex to get the man you love to do what you want is the same thing. Though he'll likely agree to do what you want to get the sex, he'll dream of a woman who genuinely desires him.

18

NEVER FAKE IT

*Help yourself and all of womankind;
tell your lover the truth about
what makes sex sublime.*

Don't fake orgasm or sexual pleasure. Many women have done it, yes, me included. Our motivations are good. We want to make our man feel talented in bed, but the consequences are harmful to men, women, and relationships as a whole.

Faking sexual pleasure misleads a man about women's bodies and sexual responses. It gives him a false sense of achievement and sets him up for future humiliation, as well as promulgating the dissemination of bad sex techniques among men. Sex is one of the few things men gossip about. The porn industry has already devastated the art of lovemaking by putting out films depicting women faking orgasms and men doing things no honest woman would enjoy. We don't need to help men become worse in bed.

Moreover, a woman shortchanges herself when she pretends to enjoy her lover's sexual techniques. She robs herself of a satisfying, juicy, soul-restoring sex life. Once duped into believing he's a champion lover, it's difficult to change his ways and teach him what you really like. Just how long will you be willing to fake pleasure in sex before you prefer skipping it? For many women, the answer is until she's got a ring on her finger.

A woman's pretending to orgasm damages the relationship. Faking pleasure, no matter how you look at it, is manipulative and dishonest. Sooner or later, the woman can't keep up the charade, or the man—like a broken clock that's right twice a day—manages to give her a real orgasm and the truth surfaces. When a man discovers he's been lied to and that he's really not a reclining rock star, it will cut him deeply. His sense of manhood, adequacy, and trust in his lover will be undermined.

Tell the compassionate truth. If the sex isn't taking you to the "Promised Land," tell him you love being with him, but things have to happen a certain way for you to climax. Show him, tell him, and moan louder when he gets it right, and go quiet when he goes off track. Be honest, patient, and gentle on his ego. You'll turn him into a sexual genius, and when he brags to his buddies about his sexual prowess, you'll be helping women everywhere.

19

THE MIND OF A MAN

*A vivid dreamer, the sensual man
creates fantasy images without consequence or plan.*

Men look at other women and think about their bodies, their
sexual nature, and what having sex with them would be like,
regardless of their love for or commitment to you. I know; what
pigs, right? Well, no. One common facet of all heterosexual
masculine men is that they have random, inconsequential sexual
thoughts about other women. They're biologically hardwired to
do this, and it has nothing to do with you or their good character.
It just happens. It doesn't mean they don't love you, that you
aren't sexy, or that your relationship is troubled. It means he's a
healthy, normal man.

Sexual thoughts that float in and out of his mind like clouds
in the sky, and are not taken seriously or acted upon, shouldn't
bother you. If they do, you have three choices: (1) Lie to yourself;
(2) Get him to lie to you; or (3) Accept it and forget about it.
If you're being honest, you'll admit that women's fantasies are
far more alarming. When women fantasize, it's generally about
a specific person and it's emotionally intense. Men are thinking
"hit it and move on," while women's imaginations are running off
into the sunset with their fantasy man.

In my relationships, I prefer a "don't ask, don't tell" approach. I know what's going on in his mind, but I don't want to be part of it. I am not a woman who likes to discuss other women with my man. I know some women who do, which is fine for them.

If my man were to check out another woman in my presence, that whole "hell hath no fury like a woman scorned" thing would break loose. I know he wouldn't appreciate the same behavior from me. I expect to be honored, adored, and the center of his attention when we are together. I give him the same honor. Adonis himself could stroll down my street holding a million dollars and singing, "Marry me, Cynthia" and I wouldn't give him a first look. Other people are far less rigid than I choose to be. What matters is that you find a way to be happy and tension-free. Be honest with yourself; figure out what you need and what you can handle. Find a solution that works for you both, and don't repress your feelings or try to repress his, for in that, you will fail.

20

BEING QUEEN

A Queen stands tall and rests on her King for support,
but when she needs to ruminate, she turns to her court.

To have the love you deserve and desire is no accident. It takes preparation, work, and lifelong effort. Construct it with high-quality ingredients, don't deviate from your recipe, and become an expert at giving a man what he needs. As the emotional leader of love, there is much you can do to stoke the passions in your king and maintain excitement and connection in your relationship. Most women readily grasp this idea and are eager to celebrate special occasions and do nice things for their lover. Yet this isn't the only way—or sometimes even the best way—to deepen your love and enliven your relationship.

To stimulate his mind and heart, let him love you while you lavish him with appreciation for all he gives you. A man's deepest needs are fulfilled by giving and being what you need. Women by nature want to do, give, and nurture, even when doing so depletes our energy or takes us away from our life's priorities. We think it's normal to sacrifice in the name of love, and we constantly search for ways to improve our relationships. This can result in exhaustion for us and prevent our men from achieving their heart's desire: to be needed. We must learn to receive the love of our men and deliberately stop doing so much to maintain our relationships. Reducing the effort we expend and relaxing into knowing we are helping our man find fulfillment this way creates the space to receive more love. Your king will feel restored, strong, and confident. His health, work, and mood all will benefit. Stop trying and doing; learn to receive your man's love, and let him feel the value of being needed by you.

Some women are uncomfortable with the idea of needing a man. They've heard me admonish women against being wholly reliant on a man, and that needing him makes them vulnerable to helpless dependency. You can be a powerful, capable queen and still need your king. It's entirely appropriate to depend on your man, provided he's worthy of your reliance. At the same time, you must maintain the ability to care for and provide for yourself, if necessary. You don't need to carry an umbrella around on a dry, sunny day, but you should keep one in your closet in case it rains. Enjoy and accept everything your king can give you. It will be good for both of you.

However, it would be best *not* to ask your man for help in the court of conversation. Men are not wired to have extended conversations that involve examining and picking apart every aspect of life. This domain is for women. Queens always have a court of ladies, and you must, too. Your court should contain women, ideally of varying ages, whom you trust, who genuinely care for you and are living lives you admire. Each element of the formula is vital. Older women are a rich resource and can share wise perspectives younger women cannot yet recognize. Let them share their life lessons, so you might avoid some of their mistakes. Your court must be trusted to keep your confidences so you can share your deepest truths and enjoy the comfort of a deep emotional connection outside of your romantic relationship. The women in your court must harbor no resentment toward you, and they must be willing to give you love, support, and their best advice.

The ladies in your court must be living or creating lives you admire, because just as it would be unwise to take diet advice from an obese person, you should never take life or relationship advice from someone whose life is miserable or has terrible relationships. When I struck out to live the life of my dreams, I had only one woman in my court. She was 73 years old and had made plenty of mistakes in her life. The important thing was she'd learned from her mistakes, she loved me, and I knew I could trust her. Her willingness to love and advise me lifted me out of the darkness and gave me a sense of direction. Later, as I established myself in my new life, I filled my court with select women who served me in many ways. They cautioned me against making bad choices and talked me down from overreacting in marital situations. My court serves as an outlet for my feelings and my need to talk things out.

My court also saves the men in my life from trying to fill this role. Men are problem-solvers who derive a tremendous sense of value and worth from figuring out what needs to be fixed and fixing it. Women are process-oriented, and though we are very capable of solving problems, we often need to spend time understanding why the problem arose and what it means to us as individuals. Most men aren't skilled at such conversations, and this is where your court can serve you and your relationship. I still have deeply emotional conversations with the man in my life, but I've learned that when I need to ruminate in the process, I must turn to my court.

PART III

THE GODDESS MOTHER

21

THE UNIVERSAL MOTHER

The world is turned by mothers' hands.

Represented as Isis, Kuan Yin, Lakshmi, Mother Mary, the Goddess Venus, and hundreds of other forms, the Universal Mother is the feminine aspect of God. She is nature and nurture, chaos and harmony. Under her rule, life flourishes, abundance abounds, and peace prevails. The Universal Mother extends unconditional love and compassion to all beings. She stands for two incontrovertible truths: one never harms another without also harming oneself, and we never suffer alone, all of creation partakes.

Modern societies have buried their connection to the Universal Mother. Only whispered rumors remain of long-standing but now lost societies that revered and worshipped women as mothers, creators, and community leaders. The wisdom of the Divine Feminine has been obscured by shortsighted self-interest, and the exploitation and destruction of nature. Masculine energy naturally seeks to conquer, build, dominate, possess, and lead. These are valuable gifts that support life and contribute to its comforts, but without the Universal Mother's heart-led guidance to balance them, destruction reigns.

Women who choose to listen to their hearts' knowing become conduits of the Universal Mother. Grounded in this insurmountable feminine strength, we empathize, uplift, connect, and heal. Through our centered coolness, understanding, and tact, we temper masculinity's liquid-hot desire to conquer, dominate, and achieve. When we embody the Universal Mother, we see the far-reaching consequences of our daily choices. We stand as guardians of nature, children, the elderly, and all who suffer. Mother-to-mother, we know there is a better solution to conflict than the giving over of our children's lives. We see our planet brimming with an abundance of food and know that no child need ever go hungry. We listen as our feminine hearts wordlessly inform us of people's turmoil, suffering, and pain. We unite the world with our innate ability to relate, comfort, and encourage. We recognize and restore our connection to the Universal Mother's power to heal. This is our sacred charge.

The Universal Mother lives in every woman. Often, she languishes undiscovered in the backwaters of a woman's heart. Those who recognize Her insurmountable power and importance are the world's greatest hope. Divided and overwhelmed by life and its stresses, we are weakened. United in the oneness of the Universal Mother, we become greater than any difficulty we face.

Eighty percent of a child's ability to learn develops by the age of eight. Worldwide, the vast majority of children spend these formative years in the care of women. Mothers, grandmothers, aunts, caregivers, and early educators all have the power to positively shift the future of humankind through the teachings imparted to children. It's our responsibility to recognize our tremendous power and direct it toward creating a better future for our people and our planet. If we fail to teach our children compassion, cooperation, and the importance of taking care of the Earth, we leave them to learn by default. If we make conscious mothering a priority, we could change our whole society in one generation.

Perhaps we are tempted to negate the significance of our womanly powers and deny the possibilities, but know that every great change in history was preceded by a time when the prospect of sweeping change seemed impossible. If apathy rules, and we view ourselves as small, inconsequential drops in a swirling sea, we remain trapped in the feminine dark age, rendered ineffective and weak. Were we to fully grasp the heavy charge put upon us, we would not tolerate the state of this world. We would work together and hold the world in the healing embrace of motherhood.

22

THE PREGNANT GODDESS

A mother incubates life,
brings it forth into the world,
sustains it on her breast, and
cradles it in the protection of her love, forever.

Through pregnancy, a woman ascends to Goddess. The wisdom of the Goddess Mother—a built-in understanding of how to nurture a child and herself—rests in all women. The vast majority of pregnancies and births pose no medical threat to mother or child, yet most births in the United States take place in a hospital with all the modern distractions to take us away from our innate knowledge. In Western culture, women are conditioned to believe that childbirth is an excruciating medical procedure, necessitating drugs, a barren setting, several educated strangers, and confinement to a bed equipped with stirrups. I bought into this myth, too. Both of my children were born in a hospital setting under bright lights and hustling doctors. I was so petrified of the pain and potential dangers that I opted for spinal anesthesia and a C-section with my first child, and an epidural VBAC (vaginal birth after Cesarean) with my second. I considered myself lucky for having emerged alive. As I've matured and explored the world, I've discovered that—like most other things related to money and control in society—women are misled into believing that to have a healthy outcome there is only one, assembly-line way.

I met Lani at a bookstore. She was a smart, self-assured recording artist, and we clicked immediately. Lani was two months pregnant, and as our friendship unfurled, I had the privilege of witnessing her blossom into motherly magnificence. Determined to honor her innate feminine wisdom, Lani refused to follow the modern prenatal and birthing regimen. Instead, she chose a doctor who practiced minimally invasive, integrative medicine that combined wisdom from other healing traditions with a medical degree. She found a birthing suite where the whole experience of labor, delivery, and healing could take place in one room and without medication. In this environment, Lani's body would be allowed to guide her labor and delivery process; she could walk, squat, and deliver in warm water.

Lani enlisted the support of a three-woman team who (collectively) had aided in the pregnancies and deliveries of over 3,000 babies. They worked with her throughout her pregnancy, not instructing, but reminding her of her feminine wisdom. They encouraged her to let her body guide her pregnancy. These wise-women made sure Lani knew that from the moment of conception until sometime after delivery, she would never be alone, and that everything she felt, thought, and did was done to the child, too. He was immersed in her energy, environment, and emotions, and his first experiences were of Lani's deepest feelings. Lani's emotional well-being was the highest priority. When she felt blue or exhausted, it was time to rest, not work. When she felt alive and full of energy, it was time to get out and be productive. Each day, time was set aside to sit in peace and commune with herself, her child, and their Creator. Over the course of her pregnancy, Lani became more conscious of her inner world and learned to help herself in times of emotional distress. She took up prenatal yoga, practiced meditation, and started painting. The normal hormonal swings presented opportunities for her to grow and practice taking care of herself and her child. As the delivery neared, the wisewomen relayed breathing techniques and shared other ways women coped with the sensations of labor long before modern medicine intervened. They told her the same feelings that created the child would ease his arrival into the world.

At full-term, Lani was a glorious expression of womanhood. Her body and mind were healthy, and even before her son was born they were emotionally bonded. I admired her and supported her choices, but I harbored trepidation because I still didn't fully trust this aspect of feminine wisdom. I doubted the possibility of drug-free and manageable labor. I feared for my friend. I wondered whether the guidance of women who made a career of ushering new lives into the world would be as competent as the hospital staff in the labor and delivery unit.

I struggled between coloring Lani's views with my fears and leaving her to chart her own maternal course, but I could not dispute the ethereal glow that emanated from her. Frequently, I sat with my hands resting on her burgeoning belly, feeling as though I'd made a physical connection to the Divine.

Lani became a confident mother, even before the birth of her son. She trusted the maternal wisdom of her ancestors to guide her and her body in nurturing the life growing inside her. When it came time to deliver, she gave in to the ancient ritual, allowing her body to express its knowing while having the freedom to move in whatever ways it wanted. Six hours later, a nascent god floated to the surface of Lani's birthing tub. He was perfect, healthy, and serene. Within moments, he nursed. Lani was invigorated and radiant. The doctor unobtrusively examined both mother and child. Satisfied with the results, she left the new family to spend their first day together undisturbed.

Though my joy for Lani's bliss cast a loving light over my world, my heart broke a little. I wished I'd known there were different ways to bring a child into the world when I gave birth. Yet, even if I had known, I would have been too afraid to choose it for myself. The medical and media machines had conditioned me (and everyone I knew) to be afraid.

Such teachings are not easy to impart, but I'm determined to share the full panoply of childbirth options with my daughter. I'm especially cautious about imprinting the belief that childbirth is a scary, agony-filled act of self-sacrifice.

Recently, while driving down a Los Angeles street, we noticed a bus stop displaying an advertisement for an upcoming reality television show about horrendous childbirths. There was a large photo of a woman in a hospital gown, drenched in sweat, shrieking, and grimacing in pain. Though I choose not to plant a negative perception of childbirth in my daughter's mind, I cannot shield her from this kind of poisonous input. The most troublesome thing is that by watching the show, women will be indirectly contributing to the funding of the show. The most malignant force in the destruction of empowered womanhood is other women, who accept as truth the myths promulgated by the media and support their dissemination.

We cannot leave the monumental decisions of our lives to cookie-cutter solutions developed and designed by people who stand to profit from our compliance. Whatever a woman chooses for herself, so long as the decision is made fearlessly and she is fully informed, is right for her.

23

A DIVINE SERVICE

*Mothers are charged with the highest assignment:
the protection and care of souls on loan from the Divine.*

There is no greater position, privilege, or achievement than mothering a child. It's a divine assignment. Mothers are given the first and highest privilege of preparing children for the journey of adult life. As women, we bear the lofty responsibility of creating an atmosphere that supports and encourages the development of children into secure, self-reliant adults, who have the tools needed to successfully pursue and fulfill their life's purpose.

Children are born with a propensity to seek goodness. They respond and blossom under the graces of affection, nurturing, closeness, and comfort. A child raised in an attentive, secure, and supportive environment has the greatest likelihood of becoming a stable, confident adult who will contribute positively to this world in some way. A mother's role is to create an atmosphere conducive for her child to become a beneficial presence. In doing so, she betters the world. This is an important legacy.

When we fulfill our purpose as mothers, we become a blessing to all of creation. We understand we are our child's steward not his creator. We know that a force greater than us formed each child for a sacred purpose and honored us with the privilege of caring for her. Inside each child is a unique set of gifts. Our greatest act is to encourage, protect, and nurture these gifts. We guard our child from ambitions fueled by ego, fear, and lack, never telling her to become an accountant, lawyer, or doctor just for the money. Happiness, personal fulfillment, and becoming the greatest expression of her true self trumps popular culture's perception of success. Wisely, we know that a child who develops her gifts, devotes herself to excellence, believes in her right to self-determination, and remains humble will find fulfilling work. We do not demand that she marry, be heterosexual, or have her own children. We understand our place as servants of creation and attach no expectation of return. We are to walk our boys and girls to adulthood, equip them with confidence and self-reliance, and release them. This is our divine service.

24

THREE GUIDING LIGHTS

Three guiding lights,
our great-grandmothers whispers remain,
illuminating the path and dissolving darkness and pain.

In preparation for writing this section, I read everything I could get my hands on about parenting and child-rearing. I talked with mothers, psychologists, coaches, and pediatricians. I also spent time listening to teenagers, and, of course, I thoroughly grilled my own children for every insight and perspective they were willing to offer. I learned that growing up today is even more challenging than it was when I grew up. Teen troubles of nearly every sort are on the rise. The Internet and media shower them with a constant deluge of images and information. The media's worship of adulterous athletes, porn video tarts turned celebrities, 20-minute marriages, and drug-addicted performers who celebrate their stupidity only reinforces the idea that nothing really matters, so long as you have money and attention. Most kids don't have money, but they can certainly get attention, especially online.

The social climate has changed, too. Sexual activity outside of courtship is increasingly common and accepted. These new pressures combined with already intense levels of adolescent stress and anxiety can be overwhelming. Most kids have no concept of quiet time alone. The chaos and constant noise masks troubles and distracts young people from discovering who they really are. Instead of taking time for reflection, they're focused on the latest cool gadget or partner they want *now*. Parents are charged with guiding their children through challenges, problems, and fears that were rare or nonexistent when they grew up. It's a harsh environment for everyone.

In my search for a solution, I came away with the distinct sense that our great-grandmothers, as limited as they might have seemed, knew something special about raising healthy children. They left behind three guiding lights that have nearly gone dark, but that could completely reverse the troubles teens face today. These three feminine gifts shrink the likelihood of depression, drug use, obesity, early sexual activity, and self-injury. They are: (1) Trust your intuition; (2) Create and uphold structure, rules, and discipline; and (3) Teach your child what it means to be a man or a woman. Let's look at these gifts more closely.

TRUST YOUR INTUITION

My friend Lisa embodies the feminine goddess in a wonderfully unique way. She is sassy and smart, a loving mother, and a gifted lawyer. What fascinates me the most about Lisa is that she is one of the most talented mystics I've met. She makes nearly every decision by what she calls "reading the energy." Before she takes on a client, goes on a trip, or makes a major purchase, she reads the energy in her body. My favorite example of this was when her son's first-grade teacher called to talk about his behavior at school. He told her that her son, Trevor, was not paying attention in class, seemed to struggle with reading comprehension, and wouldn't sit still. The teacher had already consulted with the school counselor, and together they felt certain that Trevor had

ADHD and needed medication to help him focus. He offered to set up an appointment with a local doctor who cared for many of the school's other ADHD students.

After the teacher's call, Lisa took some time to get quiet and meditate. She held the thought of Trevor having ADHD and then moved her focus down to her center, about two inches above her navel. She let it simmer, as she describes it, and then she *knew* Trevor needed something, but it wasn't medication. She *knew* he didn't have ADHD. Following her intuitive lead, she took Trevor to her family doctor, a woman who had diagnosed many legitimate ADHD cases. Lisa told her what the teacher had said. This doctor evaluated Trevor and agreed with Lisa. Trevor was a normal boy, but he had not developed the skills necessary to handle the school's intense curriculum. He wasn't ready yet. Instead of drugging a normal, active, rambunctious boy, Lisa moved Trevor to a new school that offered more opportunities for physical play and teachers who understood how to harness his attention. She followed the promptings of her intuition and overrode the professional opinions of both Trevor's teacher and the school counselor. Nearly a decade later, Trevor graduated with honors from high school, excelled on the SAT, and is bound for a top university. Lisa isn't unique in her intuitive ability. What makes her special is she actively includes it in her life. Maybe the doctor the teacher suggested would have come to the same conclusion, but every year thousands of children are misdiagnosed with ADHD and drugged unnecessarily. If Lisa hadn't followed her intuition, Trevor's life might not have turned out so well.

I've learned to trust my intuition, too, but I learned the excruciating way. It cost me more than I ever could have imagined. My former husband suffered sudden and severe headaches. We went to see his doctor, and after a few tests the doctor assured us everything was fine. He wrote a prescription for pain medication and wished us well. As we were leaving his office, a strange sensation caused me to pause in the threshold of the door. I had a split-second, but very clear, sense that the doctor was wrong. He had missed something. I turned to the doctor and said his diagnosis didn't seem right. He looked at me blankly. Grasping for something more concrete to say, I told him that my husband's pain was abnormal; it was too intense. He reassured us and suggested that we return in a few weeks if the headache persisted. On the way home, the idea of driving straight to a hospital emergency room flashed through my mind, but logical thinking shot it down as I recalled the doctor's assurance that all was well.

I chastised and judged myself for being untrusting and a "know-it-all." *How could I have the audacity to think I'm smarter than a physician?* Feeling defeated, I abandoned my inner knowing. That night, my husband suffered the devastating rupture of a brain aneurysm.

Everyone is human, including professionals, and we all make mistakes. I'm not advocating that you disregard professional advice or that you avoid doctors. It took the skill, brilliance, and bravery of dozens of talented doctors to save my husband's life that night. What I am saying is don't abandon your inner wisdom, your intuition. Don't be so terrified of being wrong, making a mistake, or offending someone that you ignore your connection to divine wisdom. It's a gift that can help you tremendously in crises and in everyday situations. Make it a practice to feel the energy in your center, the place two inches above your navel, in the center of your body. Innate wisdom, illogical knowing, and exquisite guidance emanate from there. Learn to recognize it. By all means, check your conclusions against outside sources that you trust, but never suppress, deny, or abandon what you know for sure.

CREATE AND UPHOLD STRUCTURE, RULES, AND DISCIPLINE

To stand in the second guiding light left by our great-grandmothers, we must be willing to face and overcome politically correct, overindulgent, and gender-neutral parenting practices. We must keep our "eyes on the prize," our goal of raising healthy, self-reliant, secure children. Though society has made great advances in science, social equality, and freedom, many of the most dreaded childhood maladies are on the rise: depression, anxiety, ADHD, drug use (illegal drug use is declining; prescription drug use is skyrocketing), teen sexual activity (abstinence from intercourse is increasing, but so is oral sex), obesity, self-injury, and suicide. There is a diagnosis, drug, and defined psychological disorder for every behavior. More than a few doctors note that ADHD is over-diagnosed, especially in boys. Pharmaceutical companies are building rosters of lifelong clients, and families are suffering.

Some parents, intent on being progressive, have abdicated the role of authoritarian and disciplinarian, and attempt to be best friends with their children. Though our children press for freedom, independence, and loose rules, none of these makes them happy. To parent well, you must accept that your child may not always like you in the moment, but rules and discipline show a child how much you love and value them.

When children are young, create structure; set bedtimes; enforce rules, and introduce age-appropriate, loving discipline as a part of your child's life early on. It will make the teen years much easier.

Make sure kids have downtime. Set rules limiting the use of electronic devices, assign household chores, and require respectful behavior. Get comfortable saying "No" to your child. Keep him out of environments where the risk of trouble outweighs the potential social benefits (for example, unsupervised or loosely supervised parties). Let your teens know you might show up wherever they are, at any time, and that this is entirely appropriate.

TEACH YOUR CHILD WHAT IT MEANS TO BE A MAN OR A WOMAN

To help our children understand how they fit into the world, we must recognize and embrace their differences, including gender differences. Accepting that there are inherent differences between boys and girls empowers us to guide and support them in taking ownership and control over their innate tendencies. Though it may feel uncomfortable to contradict the adamant advocates of gender-neutrality, we do our children a disservice if we ignore their built-in differences. Research proves that girls and boys are biologically, mentally, emotionally, and developmentally different.[1] Newer research indicates that children who are comfortable in their gender are psychologically better off.[2] Although this writing is specifically geared toward children who feel connected to their biological gender, children who identify differently must be embraced and supported, too.

Our great-grandmothers knew this. I think we do, too. Most mothers don't need a course on endocrinology to know there's something going on inside her son that makes him want to bang things together, knock stuff over, and use any cylindrical object as a bat or sword. We shouldn't wonder whether something went socially wrong when our daughters role-play being a mother, gravitate toward cuddly things, or when given a Superman doll host an imaginary tea party for him. Girls and boys are different. It's okay to say it out loud.

Our great-grandmothers knew child-rearing aims must be tailored to the gender of the child. Teaching your daughter the differences between the way boys and girls approach and view sex will protect her body, her emotions, and her heart. You don't want her to find out the hard way that love and sex aren't synonymous to boys. Teaching your son to channel his thrill-seeking urges and aggressive impulses into team sports and physical labor, instead of street racing and fist-fighting, could save his life.

Both genders grow up to feel secure in the world when they understand the differences between men and women and feel happy in their own skin.

NOTES

1. For a compelling, comprehensive, and science-based discussion of child gender differences and the damage caused by gender-neutral child-rearing, see Dr. Leonard Sax, *Why Gender Matters: What Parents and Teachers Need to Know about the Emerging Science of Sex Differences*, (New York: Broadway Books, 2005).

2. Jennifer Yunger, Priscilla Carver, and David Perry, "Does Gender Identity Influence Children's Psychological Well-being?" *Developmental Psychology*, 40:572-82, 2004.

25

STAY-AT-HOME GODDESS

Cradled in the arms of her mother, ever present and true,
a child is fortified to see every challenge through.

Under the weight of the daily grind, it's easy for mothers to lose sight of their monumental importance to humanity. Dirty diapers, colds, cranky outbursts, and endless tedious demands often mask the extraordinary importance of being a mother. Both society at large and mothers themselves fall prey to the fallacy that anyone can care for a child as well as a mother can. Mothers are encouraged by a culture that promotes instant gratification and material success to hand over their infants to underpaid caregivers. The consequences are grave for mother, child, and society. Even the most nurturing babysitter's care and guidance is a spectacular failure when compared to the life-affirming power of a present mother.

To grow up physically and emotionally healthy, children require deep attachments to people who love them unconditionally. Without this level of attachment, healthy development is unlikely. Infants need a consistent caregiver who holds, cuddles, and interacts with them all day long. This constant physical and emotional attention sets the foundation for feeling secure throughout life. Nature designed mothers for this role. Pregnant bodies are bombarded with bonding hormones so that mothers are profoundly driven to love, cater to, and cajole their babies. Nature fills their breasts with milk of unparalleled nutritional value and places them at the precise distance required for a newborn to see its mother's face. Supremely wise, nature designed babies to need frequent feedings to ensure the repeated physical closeness required for healthy growth.

When I brought my son home from the hospital, I was a dropout, a teen welfare mom who lived in a garage. My son's father was incarcerated. I was living the results of a tumultuous teenage life filled with bad choices. Blessedly, the moment I gave birth, my heart and maternal instincts blossomed. I resolved to do whatever was necessary to create a stable, peaceful, and nurturing environment for my son. I knew that I couldn't prevent his difficulties and challenges, but I could love, empower, and educate him, and instill in him the self-esteem necessary to make better choices than I had made.

I stayed home with my son, struggling on welfare for the first years of his life. I found another single mom to room with, and together we worked hard to make ends meet while we raised safe, happy, and loved children. We shared financial, household, and child-care responsibilities, even nursing each other's children when one of us was out for the day. We supported each other emotionally, too, serving as confidants and reassuring sisters. Most importantly, we each bonded with both children, providing the kind of tireless and devoted care that only a woman who loves a child can. It was the best I could make of a bad situation, and it was just what our children needed.

When my son approached preschool age, I felt ready to begin pursuing a career that would enable me to get off of welfare and support us. I moved in with my mother in Los Angeles, another person who loved my son. Preschool began with half-day classes, and later full days. My mother eagerly agreed to pick my son up from school every day and bring him to our home. This gave me the freedom to work. Over the next two years, I became financially self-reliant, but I still chose to continue living with my mom. I knew that no one could care for my son better than people who loved him, and nothing was more important.

I was wise enough to realize that the tender formative years of childhood are fleeting. This tiny bit of my life would set the tone for the rest of my son's life. Even when my son reached adulthood and independence, I'd still be his mother and his suffering would be mine. I viewed the sliver of time I spent devoting my life to him as a down payment on a secure, empowered, and happy future for him. During those formative years, self-sacrifice was a worthwhile and intelligent choice.

Decades later, my investment is paying off. My son is resilient, smart, self-reliant, kind, compassionate, and self-assured. He has held a job since he was 14 years old and attends one of the top universities in the country. He understands the value of being able to provide for his own needs and, one day, for his family, so his children can enjoy the benefits of being raised by people who love them, too. I was spared the terror and agony of having a teenager who behaved the way I had. The time, love, and sacrifices I made for my son during those first foundational years give me peace, happiness, and comfort today.

If you are reluctant to make changes that would allow you to be with your young child, please reconsider. Often we place our comfort, relationship desires, material wants, or career aspirations first in our lives. Babies do not obviously exhibit the harmful effects of an unstable environment. The ensuing troubles may not become apparent until much later. Think long term. Invest yourself in the first years of your child's life, and produce a lifetime of returns.

If finances are a challenge, consider moving in with a parent, other loving relative, or a close friend to share expenses and child care. When you deduct child-care costs, work-time meals, clothing, and travel expenses from after-tax income, you may discover that you net only one or two dollars an hour from keeping your job. If you must work, explore jobs that allow you to telecommute or have a flexible schedule. Challenge yourself to find creative ways to earn money so you can stay home with your child. For example, a young mother I know partnered with a local businessman who sells building materials but had no online presence. After taking only two online courses, she built and now manages his online store for him and keeps 30 percent of the gross profits. Just this one creative idea has opened a new world of flexible and profitable opportunities for her. Once her child enters school, she may go back to working outside the home, or she may choose to continue as an entrepreneur.

Do whatever it takes to give your child a loving, consistent, nurturing, and bonded caregiver. It's important to note that fathers make excellent caregivers, but many women prefer a man who provides financial support. As for primary caregivers, a parent, grandparent, or extended family relative who loves your child and understands the importance of building self-esteem and self-reliance would be ideal. At a minimum, primary caregivers must be loving and consistent in their presence.

If you are a mother for whom it is truly impossible to change lifestyles and stay at home with your child, and you have no one to help you raise your child, forgive yourself and get busy doing what you *can* do: create a new family of good people you choose. If you are totally on your own, your task is to create a community to support your child's development and your emotional welfare.

You need friendship and support, too. Look for community groups that promote connection and good values, friends who actively love their children, and people you admire. They will help you support your child, create positive influences around you both, and provide a channel for you to work out your emotional challenges. Your child should never serve this function. If you have a love interest who is not interested in being a bonded, consistent, and positive role model for your child, cut your losses and get out of the relationship immediately. Your first obligation is to your child. Unless a man is willing to join you in that duty, he's a disservice to your child and an impediment to meeting a man who *will* embrace your family. Childhood is short, but the benefits of putting your little one first will last a lifetime.

26

THE UNBREAKABLE BOND

Ten thousand tendrils of spiraling light
bind the souls of mother and child.
No force, human or divine, can tear it asunder.

Recently, I mentioned to a friend that when my son had his first sexual experience, he shared about it with me. She interrupted me mid-sentence, stunned and insistent that I tell her how my son and I have managed to create such openness in our relationship. After careful reflection, I came up with the answer: Since the day he was born, I've cultivated intimacy.

My desire as a new mother was to create and maintain a resilient bond that tethered us together, despite the challenges of age, time apart, or physical distance. This form of intimacy is the greatest preventative force against your child making harmful choices, and the most magnificent reward of mothering. It repays all the work and sacrifice of child-rearing, and pours infinite love into the hearts of both parent and child.

The cornerstone of maintaining intimacy with your child is making sure they know you love them under all circumstances and conditions. They should know this like they know their name. Before either of my children could assemble sentences, I began repeating this mantra, "No matter what happens, even when I'm upset, I love you and this will never change."

I continue to say it every now and then. But you won't convince a child by words alone; they're too smart to be fooled. The words gain strength through your behavior and actions. Here are some fundamental ways to establish solid intimacy.

BE PRESENT WHEN YOU'RE TOGETHER

When you spend time with your child, put down the electronic gadgets, papers, and other distractions. Show your little one what it means to spend quality time together. Point out the fact that you're turning off your phone and putting the newspaper away because that's what people who really want to connect with each other do. You'll appreciate this later, when your teen wants to implant an iPad into their forearm. Set the habit early and live it yourself.

COMMUNICATE

Talk, share, and explain everything, even to your youngest child. When no topic is off-limits, it lays the foundation for open communication later in life. Keep the content age-appropriate. Answering your nine-year-old daughter's questions about sex at a level she can understand will make your more in-depth conversation with her much easier when she's 14. It also sets you up to be a confidant and resource. If you don't know the answer to your child's question, say so and then look it up. Show her that not knowing an answer is okay, and that knowing how to *find* the right answer is what counts.

ACCEPT THEM FOR WHO THEY ARE

Allow them to follow their desires, provided they cause no harm to themselves or others. In practice, this means that regardless of their religious preference, sexual orientation, or an unrelenting passion to become a basket weaver instead of a doctor, you love them. You must share your truth, including when you disagree with their choices, but do so in a loving way without laying on guilt or shame.

NEVER JUDGE FEELINGS; FOCUS ON HEALTHY BEHAVIOR

Create a safe haven for communication. Children, like adults, feel jealousy, sadness, pain, hatred, and frustration. Never tell a child they shouldn't feel a certain way or they should stop crying; it alienates them. Instead, explain appropriate behaviors. Let them express how they feel. If you don't want to hear it, tell them, "I love you and I'm going to let you get out your feelings *in your room*. I'll be close by if you need me."

CREATE A SAFE-ZONE FOR COMMUNICATION

Your child must know that he can express *anything* to you, so long as it's done respectfully. Parents can create insurmountable communication barriers by chastising and criticizing their children's opinions. Offending ideas and behaviors rarely resolve under criticism. Instead, children hide them from parents to avoid further criticism. Many children rebel against parental admonitions as a way of demonstrating autonomy. This can result in difficult challenges as children reach adolescence. Use the safe-zone of communication to explain the negative impacts of your child's opinion or behavior. Explain the consequences and your responsibility as a parent to uphold values and discipline when required. In this zone of safe communication, both parent and child can tell the truth.

TREAT YOUR CHILDREN AS INDIVIDUALS WITH RIGHTS, VALUE, AND IMPORTANCE

Society relegates children to the status of lesser beings. Both my children have told me that when they're on their own in public, they notice many adults nudging children aside without apology. This negates their value. Parents can offset this experience. Listen to your children's ideas, and ask them why they believe the things they do. Acknowledge and admire them when they come up with something interesting. Never dismiss them as small, incapable, or annoying. Tell them they are going to be great adults who create good for themselves and others. See the healthy traits and confidence in them now that you'd like to show up later.

INSTILL RULES OF CONDUCT BEFORE THEY'RE NEEDED

With issues such as sex, drugs, and other potentially dangerous ideas, state the household rules and discuss them long before adolescence. Just like religious beliefs, you can program social mores and healthy lifestyle choices into young children. In my home, you may not date until after high school, you may never have sex outside of a committed relationship, there is no smoking or drug use allowed, and everyone must pull the weight they are capable of carrying. I spent countless hours talking with my 5- to 11-year-old children about these rules; whenever anyone we knew suffered the negative consequences of breaking them, they became examples for learning. Although my children appeared disinterested or as though they weren't paying close attention, they didn't miss a thing. Children record what you say, but even more so, what you do. Choose wisely. Don't program them by default.

APOLOGIZE

When you make a mistake—and we all do—apologize. Do it swiftly and completely. No excuses. No diverting blame. Explain where you went wrong, what you wish you had done, and what you're going to do to repair any damage. This is a powerful act. Not only does it model exemplary human behavior, it fosters trust.

DON'T BE A BRAT

There is no place in loving relationships for guilt, the silent treatment, temper tantrums, or other displays of emotion aimed at manipulating your child or anyone else. This is toxic behavior that trains your child to engage in it and be attracted to it. If this is you, stop it.

AVOID GOSSIP

Talking negatively about friends, family, or community members who aren't present and able to respond sends a harmful message to everyone, especially your children. It tells them that you are capable of smiling in people's faces and then betraying them. Gossiping about family members (as so many people do) plants the idea that it's okay to betray people you claim to love. This undermines a child's ability to trust. There is a dramatic difference between using real-life examples to teach your child about life's consequences and trashing someone else to make yourself feel superior.

USE POSITIVE LABELS

Your words are powerful, and they shape your child's view of herself. Thoughtless utterances of words like stupid, fat, dumb, lazy, bad, mean, space case, and dork, and even seemingly benign words such as jolly, round, blondie, or stocky, can trigger negative beliefs. Tell your child she's beautiful, wonderful, brilliant, and a joy to spend time with. If there is a condition that needs attention, be sure to point out that she is not the condition, and together you're going to work to improve it. My children attend academically demanding schools, and I've made sure they know that they are not their grades. They are valuable in and of themselves, and I expect them to do their work well and on time, and earn the best grades they can.

CREATE A THIRD ENTITY

Teach your child that your relationship is a separate entity created by the two of you. It requires attention, care, and maintenance to thrive. Lying, disrespect, and poor treatment destroy relationships—honesty, caring, and nurturing encourage them to grow. Even young children grasp this concept well. They understand that the relationship will care for you both and provide a lifetime of safety, connectedness, and joy.

LET GO, AGAIN AND AGAIN

Don't fall into the dark side of mothering and clip your child's wings. Understand that the ultimate success of a mother is not evidenced by what her child chooses to do with his life, or how physically close or emotionally dependent he is on her. Success is producing a child who is self-reliant, emotionally secure, and a beneficial presence in the world. In order for your child to soar, you have to be willing to let him fly—away from you. The gift of establishing true intimacy is that he'll remain connected and eager to share his adventures with you.

WALK YOUR TALK

Instill confidence and trust by living the views and values you teach. To have a happy, honest, hardworking, emotionally stable, self-reliant child who brings good into the world, become that kind of adult. They won't do what you say; they'll do what you do.

Your job as a mother is to provide unconditional love, discipline, and understanding of consequences, keeping in mind they are leaves of the same branch. Love your children no matter what they do, hold them accountable for their choices, and allow them to bear the consequences of their actions, because you love them. Feeding their spirit with love and allowing them to fall and get back up nurtures the fortitude and resilience required to handle the inevitable losses and sorrows of life.

27

BE A SHAPE-SHIFTER

A mother is water, soothing, healing, and pure,
taking the form required to cure.

As a woman who loves without limits, my goal is to create an environment that fosters respect, admiration, and connections free of guilt and obligation so my children want to be emotionally close with me, even after they "leave the nest." Creating this sort of environment requires me to take conscious control over something that women are innately gifted at: shape-shifting.

Mothers are natural shape-shifters. We can instantly change from caring nurses to firm teachers to supportive friends to disciplinarians; we bring to life whatever form the situation requires. My son has held a job teaching Tae Kwon Do since he was 14. At 16, he became frustrated and wanted to quit. I felt that keeping the job was best for him, because it taught him self-reliance, gave him financial freedom, enhanced his body, and would distinguish him when he applied to college. Though my impulse was to tell him outright what he should do, I knew that would create two sides to the issue, his and mine. When he came to me to talk about resigning, I consciously shifted into the role of counselor. I argued both sides of the issue, explaining that by resigning he'd have more time for friends, relaxation, and working out. His grades might improve, and how nice it would be to have him home more. This was all true. Then, in the same tone of fairness, I shared the other side, the things he'd be giving up and the potential consequences. I told him what I would choose, but I also assured him that I'd love and support him in whatever choice he made. Empowering him with the freedom to choose and the responsibility for his choice improved his sense of self-confidence and dissolved any potential rebellion against me. He chose to keep his job and maintained it until college.

Conscious shape-shifting is an art. Every situation is different. When my son was much younger, around the age of 10, he was a red belt in Tae Kwon Do and had come up against a boy who intimidated him. The boy, Joe, would sit across from my son before sparring matches and roar and gnash his teeth. They were well matched in skill and size, but Joe's menacing undermined my son's confidence. He was afraid and adamant about quitting Tae Kwon Do altogether. I talked with the lead instructor, a man I knew well and trusted, and he assured me that Joe was the right opponent for my son. He said the worst thing anyone could do is let him quit under the present circumstances. I talked with my son lovingly and encouraged him to stick with it. It wasn't enough. He refused to go back to class. Against nearly every maternal desire to protect him, I shifted into the uncomfortable role of rigid authoritarian. I knew that the effects of letting my son quit because someone got under his skin could create a pattern of buckling under adversity. I made the lead instructor promise me that if I forced my son to come to class he would give him reassurance, support, and close supervision.

Allowing your child to face conflict and manage the consequences of his behavior is a crucial component of motherhood. Remember, whatever your role needs to be under any circumstance, the main thing is to love and empower your child. Allowing children to deal with the results of their choices is a loving behavior. Our inclination is to shield our children from difficulty. When danger, destruction, or harm is present, we should protect them; but when you feel tempted to intervene so your child won't have to grapple with consequences, step back. Let them miss the dance, sit out the season, pay for damages, confess, and apologize. Let it happen and love them through it. Let your child learn when he's young and the stakes are low. This may be the greatest gift of all. On top of all the benefits to your children, letting them learn responsibility and accountability will foster their respect for you, which is a key component of intimacy.

28

LITTLE GODS AND GODDESSES

He's a burning fire; she's a drenching rain;
both are capable of magic, creation, and gain.

As a post–feminist revolution's disciple of political correctness, I was taught that boys and girls are inherently the same, and the only reason we behave differently is because we were socialized by a sexist society to adopt artificial gender stereotypes. Nonsense. Socialization has an influence in child development and gender perception, yet there is ample evidence that girls and boys are inherently different.

From early moments in utero, male and female brains develop differently. The bundle of nerves that connects the right and left hemispheres of the brain is denser in girls.[1] Once born, boys use compartments of their brains to complete a task; girls use more of the whole brain, and their brains remain active longer after the task is complete.[2] Boys' brains are built to excel at spatial tasks early (for example, building with blocks); girls excel at verbal communication and reading years before boys.[3] Girls are able to multitask and analyze everything—boys focus and master physical tasks, often with dogged determination.[4] Young boys have shorter attention spans than girls of the same age and take in less sensory data from their environment.[5] Girls perceive the totality of their environment without effort, including the people, things, emotions, and behaviors that surround them.[6]

Hormones and neurotransmitters amplify these differences.[7] Boys' brains are awash in testosterone, a hormone that encourages aggressive behavior.[8] Girls' brains contain high levels of estrogen, a hormone that inhibits aggressive behavior.[9] Boys seek action over affection. Girls seek continuous touch. The research detailing the fundamental differences in male and female development, thinking processes, and emotional makeup is extensive and plentiful. They are different. Understanding these differences and finding ways to harness and channel their strengths contributes to raising healthy, well-adjusted, and successful children.

Like adult men and women, boys and girls are equals. Neither is superior; both are capable, strong, and remarkable. Boys are not innately better at math, and girls are not better at reading. They develop these skills at different ages and rates.[10] Healthy girls and boys who receive an education tailored to the distinct ways their brains function and learn can enjoy and master all subjects.[11] The gender-neutral approach to education deprives both sexes of their best environment for learning.[12] It presents material in ways that often deter one gender from embracing a subject. For example, most boys will develop a love of reading if allowed to read non-fiction war stories and adventures about masculine men.[13] Similarly, you can teach girls geometry in the context of dramatic mystery, rife with rich characters in real-life situations, and they'll master it.[14]

We must support our children in learning to wield their strengths with intelligence and compassion. They need practice, kind guidance, and non-judgmental feedback to learn to positively express all aspects of themselves. A child who fails to learn how to channel and harness their innate urges becomes an ill-equipped adult.

Discouraging your daughter from fantasizing about being a mother or homemaker contradicts a part of her essence and sets her up for inner conflict. Her natural urge to nurture should be encouraged, because it's essential to her well-being and of great future value to society.

To shame boys who exhibit aggressive behavior deprives them of developing self-trust and the ability to control their inherent attraction to physical force and dominance. The risk in removing supervised and safe expression of aggression from boys is that they never learn to stand their ground or to channel the fire within. This innate urge does not evaporate, it smolders.

Allowing boys to be boys, and girls to be girls, does not mean we limit their expression to gender-specific roles. The authentic inherent qualities of an individual child trump all general gender tendencies. Allow your son to play dolls and dress up if that's what he wants. Encourage your daughter to roll in the dirt and play cops and robbers if that's what brings her joy. Follow your child's lead. The healthiest, most confident, and self-reliant adult is one whose inherent strengths and specific tendencies were honored, nurtured, celebrated, and channeled in a positive direction as a child.

NOTES

1. See Reuwen Achiron, Shlomo Lipitz, and Anat Achiron's paper "Sex-Related Differences in the Development of the Human Fetal Corpus Callosum: *In Utero* Ultrasonographic Study," in *Prenatal Diagnosis*, vol. 21: pp. 116-120 (2001).

2. See Michael Gurian and Patricia Henley with Terry Trueman's *Boys and Girls Learn Differently!* (San Francisco: Jossey-Bass, 2001).

3. See Jean Christophe Labarthe's paper "Are Boys Better Than Girls at Building a Tower or a Bridge at 2 Years of Age?" in *Archives of Disease in Childhood*, vol. 77: pp. 140-144 (1997); and Michael Gurian and Patricia Henley with Terry Trueman's *Boys and Girls Learn Differently!* (San Francisco: Jossey-Bass, 2001).

4. See Michael Gurian and Kathy Stevens's paper "With Boys and Girls in Mind," in *Educational Leadership*, vol. 62: pp. 21-26 (2004).

5. See Jennifer Bingham Hull's article "The Lost Boys" in *Parenting Magazine*, pp. 144-148 (2003); and Alison McCook's "Why a Mans Ouch Is Different Than a Woman's," *Reuters,* December 20, 2002

6. See Michael Gurian and Kathy Stevens's paper "With Boys and Girls in Mind," in *Educational Leadership*, vol. 62: pp. 21-26 (2004).

7. See Michael Gurian and Patricia Henley with Terry Trueman's *Boys and Girls Learn Differently!* (San Francisco: Jossey-Bass, 2001).

8. See Leonard Sax's *Why Gender Matters* (New York: Broadway Books, 2005).

9. See Michael Gurian and Patricia Henley with Terry Trueman's *Boys and Girls Learn Differently!* (San Francisco: Jossey-Bass, 2001).

10. See Harriet Hanlon, Robert Thatcher, and Marvin Cline's paper "Gender Differences in the Development of EEG Coherence in Normal Children," in *Developmental Neuropsychology*, vol. 16(3): pp. 479-506 (1999).

11. For a comprehensive discussion of the benefits of tailoring education to the learning style of each gender, please go to the National Association for Single Sex Public Education Website: http://www.singlesexschools.org.

12. See Leonard Sax's *Why Gender Matters* (New York: Broadway Books, 2005).

13. Ibid.

14. Ibid.

PART IV

VENUS AT WORK

29

THE MANDATE: BE CAPABLE, COMPETENT, AND FEMININE

A woman complete and fully expressed
must always be able to feather her nest.

Whenever the concept of being feminine comes up in the context of careers, women jump to the conclusion that being feminine means being powerless, subservient, and weak. It doesn't. In order to freely chart the course of your life, you must be capable of providing for yourself. Even if you make the admirable and generous choice to create a career of homemaking and child-rearing, you must know that you can care for yourself. No matter how secure your marriage or life appears to be, it's vital that you understand your financial situation and develop and maintain the ability to provide for yourself and your children. It's unwise, and sometimes self-harming, to have no other option than relying on someone else for your financial support. Love and trust your man with all your heart, but love yourself by making sure you have the skills, knowledge, and ability to handle the unexpected, if necessary. Life is unpredictable. Divorce, death, disability, and disaster are real and common occurrences. No one is immune.

I married a loving man who was eager to provide for our family and me. He earned a very large income and was extraordinarily generous. It was common for him to give me gifts of cars, jewelry, and trips. One Valentine's Day, he even wrote me a note giving me every possession he had. It was his way of expressing his absolute devotion to our marriage and honoring me. He was young, successful, and trustworthy. We were extraordinarily happy and never doubted that we'd spend our lives together enjoying our abundance. Yet, in a single moment, everything changed. An artery spontaneously ruptured in my husband's brain, and the bleeding washed away his memory, personality, ability to work, and our marriage. There was nothing we could have done better in our marriage; we loved each other and cherished being together. Our sudden ending was beyond our control or influence. That day, I went from being stay-at-home mom, wife, and leisurely entrepreneur, to solely responsible parent, interim CEO of his businesses, caregiver, and sole debtor to our mortgage.

Blessedly, I had skills and abilities. I had a law degree and a real estate license. Through the years, I'd maintained my connections in real estate, design, acting, personal development, travel, and cultures. This gave me a range of options. I dressed myself up, walked into one of the highest-grossing real estate agencies in the world, and became a real estate broker. It was a job that would allow me the flexibility to be with my children while I made money and regained my footing. I worked in real estate for nearly three years, as I built my personal development and business consulting practice on the side. I spent much of the time terrified of what calamity might arise in the next moment, but it could have been much worse. I managed to keep my home and provide continued stability for my children. None of it was easy, but I was spared the lasting suffering so many women endure when tragedy happens unexpectedly.

Accept this as a non-negotiable mandate: Whatever your life plans might be, you must be able to take care of yourself and your children. If you are currently reliant on someone else and have not developed the skills to provide for yourself, start equipping yourself with skills, abilities, and interests immediately. You don't need a law degree or other lofty education. Choose something you're interested in and learn about the careers and businesses that relate to it. Take classes, read, volunteer, consider starting a home-based business, or find part-time work that allows you to telecommute. Get connected to something that interests you and provides career opportunities. Do it now! You may never need or want to work again, but your life will be exponentially enhanced by knowing that you can.

30

THE ACCURATE MEASURE
OF A WOMAN'S CAREER

Leaving motherhood
out of a woman's career experience
is like excluding the horizon from a sunrise.

As women have moved into the workforce, professional careers have become an important measure of personal success and fulfillment. Equal pay, promotions, titles, and employment rights remain concerns, because women have yet to achieve the same levels of reward and recognition as men. Although tremendous advancements have been made, women who choose to bear and raise children face limits on their career progress, which leaves men, still, with the upper hand. This causes many women to feel slighted, as though their time spent raising children who enhance the world is somehow less significant than bringing home the biggest paycheck.

Instead of valuing the totality of work—and parenting *is* work—they see successful performance through the eyes of men. Men measure career success as an accounting of dollars, titles, social status, and personal satisfaction. Parenting is rarely a consideration in the male measure of success.

Mothers need to be measured on a different scale. For a mother to measure her professional success and fail to include motherhood diminishes its value and makes the term "stay-at-home mom" mean little more than babysitter. Under the current backward thinking, the babysitter is often assigned more value than the stay-at-home mom because our society values efforts to acquire money over non-material achievements.

Much the way that we have different criteria and measures for women in competitive sports, we must assess professional success using accurate and appropriate standards for women. Time spent as the CEO of "New Life Creation and Nurturing," a.k.a. "Mom," must be given its proper weight. No vocation demands mastery of so many complex skills. No profession requires a greater commitment of time and unwavering responsibility. Involved parenting equips a woman with the ability to handle countless complex logistical, emotional, financial, and intellectual challenges under the pressures of exhaustion, sleep deprivation, isolation, and frustration. A mother becomes a master of endurance, delayed gratification, perseverance, and conflict resolution. Her innate wisdom and intuition blossoms—she hears the inaudible and sees the unseen. In motherhood, she can learn every skill required to own or manage a successful business.

31

DOMESTIC GODDESS

Graduate of an institution greater than any other,
a business is blessed by a stay-at-home mother.

There is a critical distinction between mothers who emerge from parenting capable of running a successful business or other career, and women who are lost when their children leave home. How a stay-at-home mother spends her time shapes her being, not just the children's. A woman who embodies the negative stereotype of stay-at-home mother as maid and babysitter, watches endless TV, and obsesses over cosmetics and cleaning products misses the sublime opportunity to grow her life, career, and womanly power. I know the slouching stay-at-home mom and the goddess-mother well, because I've been both.

I became pregnant with my first child after dropping out of school. Unemployed, I surrounded myself with young welfare moms from "the 'hood." Together, we spent our days in front of the television arguing over diaper absorbency, spot-removing power, and just how high oven-baked rolls could rise. A typical day began with some sort of packaged food, a bath, vacuuming, dusting, watching the *Price is Right* followed by the *Young and the Restless*, lunch (more packaged food), *All My Children, General Hospital, Oprah*, dinner, and the local news. Occasionally, a trip to the park or mall was thrown in for exercise.

By my third trimester, I was a fully converted, media-controlled "Mommy-maton." I ate what the advertisers told me to, idolized the blissfully happy commercial moms, and fell asleep at night wondering what Erica Kane would do tomorrow about her latest romantic fiasco. I missed her terribly on the weekend. My place, a garage, was spotless. The scent of fields of fake flowers filled the air, just like the moms on television. My body was heavy and doughy in a way that had nothing to do with being pregnant, even as I longed to look like the airbrushed girls in the cosmetics ads. My ability to do math in my head was diminished, and I felt sluggish and tired all the time, too.

Having no real identity of my own, no interests, and no goals beyond the next bit of entertainment and cleaning, I languished. I was financially destitute, but, most days, the constant barrage of jingles, colors, drama, and chatter pouring from the television distracted me from life's struggles. My friends shared in the delusion. We had no dreams, just a bevy of unattended problems, and we never even thought about the women we might want to become.

Thankfully, when I felt the warm weight of my son's body lying across my chest, a part of me broke free. The energy of the Goddess Mother surged in my heart and triggered my own rebirth. The importance of each moment, the preciousness, and the fleeting nature of time all became clear. I turned away from the other moms in my group and set out to create a life that challenged my new son and myself to be our very best.

I took small, incremental steps toward a better life, first sharing a home with another single mom and then moving to Los Angeles so my mother could help me love and care for my son while I took a part-time job. When my son turned three, he entered preschool and I started a business that allowed me to be with him after school. Our television sat cold as we explored everything from birds to skyscrapers. We took trips, studied languages, and made new friends. When my son started kindergarten, I entered law school. The following summer, I married a wonderful man and soon after became pregnant. This pregnancy was completely different. The days of obsessing over how to make my already white laundry even whiter were over. I spent my second pregnancy immersed in the wonder of creation. When my daughter was born, I took a year off to be a 100 percent domestic goddess. Fortunately, my new husband was more than happy to carry the load. I resolved that my year at home would be rich with growth for both my children and me. Instead of watching television, we listened to Mozart and visited gardens and museums. I wrote in my journal every day and bought a set of workout DVDs and a home study course in French. I took my children to the beach, made crafts, and played in the mud. I talked with them about everything we encountered. My time at home was not just about tending to the needs of children—I was growing competent individuals, myself included.

Through it all, I held in my heart and mind an image of the woman I wanted to be: educated, fun, secure, worldly, loving, successful, kind, and empowered. Holding her in focus created these qualities in me. Now, I am more this woman than ever, and my children are self-reliant, compassionate, and independent thinkers.

My career as a mother instilled more ability, expertise, knowledge, and wisdom in me than any professional position. Motherhood presents the opportunity to catapult oneself above the ranks of textbook knowledge and workplace experience to the status of a fully evolved leader, capable of handling all aspects of successful business management. Whether I am giving a talk, negotiating a transaction, managing a project, building a brand, or writing a book, I rely more on skills perfected in the workshop of motherhood than I do my education or professional work experience. I credit my work as mother with every success I achieve. Perhaps, one day, society will see the true value of motherhood, too.

32

A CAREER FIT
FOR A GODDESS

*Success, joy, and purposeful work are inextricably entwined.
They flourish abundantly in the Garden of the Divine.*

A fulfilling career can be an extraordinary part of a woman's life and purpose. Yet few women discover their perfect work. Many of us spend over 2,000 hours a year in positions we don't enjoy. The highlights of many work/life experiences are clocking out and vacation time. This is a tragic waste of time, life force, and gifts.

Imagine looking forward to working each day and feeling good about the contribution you've made as well as the money you've earned. This is a reality for some women, and it can be for you, too.

Many people believe you can't make a living doing what you love. *You can.* The greatest opportunity for financial abundance and personal fulfillment lies in choosing a career you are passionate about and using it to serve others. Service does not require discomfort or sacrifice to be worthwhile. The crucial element of meaningful service is the consciousness you hold. Giving from a consciousness of lack doesn't fool the universe—lack will return to you, regardless of the magnitude of the gift. This is why it's so important to love your work and how you give. To create flowing abundance, you must give with a joyful heart. When you combine your talents and passions, life will become pleasurable and rewarding, and the returns will be exponentially increased.

You may struggle to identify your true interests and loves. Happy childhood moments often contain the clues to latent passions. All children have innate gifts that can translate to fulfilling careers as adults. Some love to talk and connect, like therapists, coaches, teachers, and speakers. Many children come alive when expressing themselves through painting, sculpting, drafting, or singing. Others feel deep satisfaction from solving problems, helping others heal, or building physical structures. There are numerous adult professions related to each interest. Every heart-based passion can be connected to a career. You may love an activity, such as dancing, but have no talent for it as a career. However, you can apply your skills to a career that is connected to dance but more suited to your abilities, such as becoming a performing arts marketer, agent, or production manager. Stay true to your interests and become an eager learner and expert at what you love. You'll be amazed at the people and opportunities that find you when you actively follow your bliss.

As you pursue your ideal career, there may be times when you need to take what I call "survival jobs." We live on the physical plane, after all, and to translate the energy of our dreams into form can take time. Yet, with a destination in mind and an understanding that the survival job is temporary, you can avoid feelings of boredom and despair, and allow your vision to pull you toward your dreams.

Cheryl grew up loving sports. As a child, she tracked the statistics of every hockey, football, baseball, and basketball team. She read all the sports magazines and snatched the athletic section from her uncle's newspaper daily. Cheryl was a good, but not great, athlete. She swam, played basketball, ran track, and competed in the high jump. As she grew into womanhood, her body became less athletic. By the time she was in college, she no longer felt physically competitive, but her love of sports was still strong. To her, the idea of continuing her life involved in sports and being paid for it was the pinnacle of success.

Work, like life, will always present difficulties. A person in a job they love will have the tenacity required to persevere and succeed. Passion and commitment to your purpose acts as a safety-jacket—it buoys and sustains you.

Against her parents' wishes, Cheryl majored in communications. She also started writing a sports blog and applied for an unpaid internship at a local sports radio station. In her spare time, she volunteered to raise funds for charity functions held by sports TV and radio stations, and by super-star athletes. Times were tough. Cheryl worked in a sandwich shop, took out student loans for college, and spent hours working to write articles she hoped sports fans would enjoy. At one time, she had only enough money to eat beans and rice. Cheryl reflects on this time as one of the best in her life. Her life revolved around her passion. Her love of sports carried her through.

Soon, the charity event hosts began to recognize her at their functions. Her infectious enthusiasm for sports attracted the attention of a few high-profile sports agents and television producers. They followed her blog and shared her most entertaining articles within their social circles. When Cheryl graduated, she was offered a job as a sports reporter at one of the nation's preeminent stations.

Today, Cheryl reports stories that encourage teamwork, good sportsmanship, and striving for excellence. She is an inspiration to children and sports enthusiasts everywhere. Cheryl is earning a great income for work she would be willing to do for free. This is true success.

33

UNLEASHING DIVINE POWER

Behind every great woman is her
True Self: a divine emanation.

Self-doubt holds women in tight, but seemingly safe, corners. In truth, to doubt your divine gifts is an insult to Creation. You are only a conduit. Get out of the way. Awaken to the truth that you are here on purpose. You are a magnificent being created by the same energy that created every person you've ever admired. To nurture, grow, and express the best in you is to honor Creation. This benefits not only you, but also every other person confined to their personal corner of doubt. When you become your best, you are a beacon of possibility, a living inspiration. When you play small, your suffering is not limited to you. It touches everyone.

Don't wait! You're already worthy. You are enough. Acknowledge your feelings of fear and unworthiness and press on. Do what you love. If you dream of owning a successful business, write a business plan and get started now, whatever your circumstances. Start as small as you have to, just start.

Don't be stopped by what others may think. A goddess never allows society or ego to stop her from following her bliss. Your goal is to fully utilize and express your talents, capacities, and potential. In describing self-actualized people, Abraham Maslow (a titan of psychology) wrote, "The highest quality that a human being can reach is to be independent of the good opinion of others." I practice living from this tenet and have revised it to read: "Self-actualization is being independent of the good or bad opinion of others." After years of effort, I have come to a place where, with few exceptions, I think for myself and trust my heart, Spirit, and intuition to guide me.

I encourage you to write down your own definition of self-actualization, and also your intention to live a heart-led life. Place it somewhere you'll see it often. It takes courage and bravery to refuse to live out the desires of your parents, peers, or community. You may even lose their favor or respect, for a time. Fret not. When you succeed in your passionate purpose, praise will come—although as a self-actualized woman, you won't need it.

There is a career for every passion, and all work can be used to serve others and society. No path is too small if it enlivens you. Gardeners, lawyers, artists, doctors, businesswomen, homemakers, athletes, chefs, pet groomers, and countless other professions, when aligned with purpose and love, possess the potential for abundance, growth, and service.

Play to your strengths and forget about your weaknesses. It's nearly impossible to turn inherent weaknesses into excellence. You can be bad at something and get better, but you will probably never be great. The world is full of people who are considered good at their jobs, but very few attain excellence—those who do receive the greatest reward and recognition. To cultivate excellence, focus on enhancing your strengths. Chances are high that what you are naturally good at intersects with your passions.

Improving from weaknesses and mediocrity can only serve you up to the point that you become competent in basic written expression, mathematics, and a general understanding of worldly function. Beyond that, there is not enough benefit to justify the effort when you could channel your energy to going from good to great. If you are a terrible writer but you love math, drop your creative writing class and hire a math tutor.

Accept that you are a unique creation, an amalgamation of gifts and attributes that exist in no one else. Your essence is alive and ever flowing within you. Tap into it and go with (not against) the current. The world needs your gifts.

34

THE MIRROR OF MONEY

*Only when the flower recognized her own splendor
did the world tell her she was beautiful.*

Do you routinely, and for no rational reason, charge less than fair market value for your work or services? Do you take less so someone else can have more? Do you accept gifts and compliments graciously or deflect them? Are you always broke?

Our financial picture is a reflection of our inner views about our worthiness and whether or not we believe we deserve abundance.

Sara was struggling financially and wanted to make more money, so she came to me for help. Sara runs a busy bookkeeping service in Los Angeles, but she had to let her assistant go because she couldn't afford to pay her. Sara said her business was suffering because her clients were under financial strain, and she was trying to help them by offering discounts and undercharging. As a result, she could barely cover her expenses. On top of that, she'd made several loans to friends in financial trouble who hadn't paid her back.

I took a look at Sara's financials and discovered that she'd been charging the same rates for seven years, and they were far lower than any other full-service bookkeeper's rates. I asked her to raise her rates to fair market value, and she balked, citing the spiraling economy and her fear of losing all of her clients. I offered her the following truths:

144

EVERYONE DESERVES FAIR PAY

No one should work for less than the market value of her work. Check inside. Ask yourself, *Should they?* When I ask this question and it's applied to anyone other than the person who is undercharging, they always say, "Of course not." We all know there is something wrong with paying someone less than they deserve. Though some people feel like they've won something when they manage to under-pay, this is not the energy you want to put out to the Universe, unless you are ready to have it returned to you in spades.

ABUNDANCE IS EVERYWHERE

Left to itself, the Universe is friendly and flows in unbounded abundance. The ocean doesn't count how many waves hit shore, an orange tree doesn't reach its quota and stop production, and the sun doesn't shine only on the people who "deserve" it. Nature's abundance knows no limit. Align your thoughts with this truth rather than the manic-depressive sways of the economy. Many people succeed no matter what the economic conditions. Include yourself in this group.

YOU MUST GIVE TO RECEIVE

Abundance flows in a cycle similar to breathing. You must inhale to exhale. You must also be willing to receive in order to give. Hindering either action blocks the flow and results in deficiency. The entire cycle is strengthened when you and your customer or employer exchange fairly and joyfully.

YOUR SUCCESS HELPS OTHERS

You cannot suffer enough to make other people successful. The idea that by living small or joining another in struggle we somehow help them overcome their suffering is nonsense. The best way to help another person be successful is to model successful behavior. Charging fair prices and delivering excellent work on time is the way to teach others about success.

PEOPLE VALUE WHAT THEY PAY FOR

Paying for a product or service instills in the buyer an affirmative belief in the value of the purchase. People do not value what they get at a deep discount.

Sara's eyes lit up. She understood the truth of the ideas I'd shared. But within moments, her anxiety returned. She confessed the most limiting and pervasive belief of all: she was afraid to raise her prices because she felt unworthy of earning more. She didn't believe it was "okay" for her to have an abundant income, and she is not alone in thinking this way.

The single biggest barrier to women receiving equal pay for equal work is that deep down many women don't believe they deserve it. We all grew up programmed to both want and fear money. The majority of women receive messages of scarcity and negativity about money. Consider the following common statements: "She's a gold digger; she only married him for the money; she doesn't need to work; girls aren't that smart, so you better look for a waitress job when you get out of high school."

Money is energy, and it's neutral. It's not good or bad, and it doesn't go to or away from so-called "good" or "bad" people. What we think of it and how we use it gives money its only meaning. Know that you are just as deserving of financial comfort and abundance as anyone who has ever lived. Trust yourself to handle money well. Begin cultivating a friendly relationship with money by following these practices:

ACCEPT ALL GIFTS AND COMPLIMENTS GRACIOUSLY

Smile as you look the gift giver in the eyes and thank them. Know that you are thanking the Universe for using that person to give you a gift. If the gift isn't to your liking, donate it later to someone who will love it.

PICTURE YOURSELF ENJOYING ABUNDANCE

Spend 15 minutes a day visualizing yourself receiving and taking advantage of opportunities, and attracting and easily accepting abundance. If you struggle with visualization, find a guided meditation on prosperity.

CHANGE YOUR PERCEPTION OF WHAT YOUR WORK OR PRODUCT IS WORTH

Don't make decisions out of negative programming or fear. Be objective. Whether you are employed by a company or run your own business, study three positions, businesses, or products that are similar to yours and make sure that your rates, salary, or prices are competitive. Update your research from time to time.

ASK FOR MORE

A research study by Linda C. Babcock, Ph.D., professor of economics at Carnegie Mellon University and director of the Program for Research and Outreach on Gender Equity in Society, states that one main reason why women earn less money and receive fewer promotions than men is because we do not ask for as much, or ask as often.[1] Asking feels uncomfortable. It goes against our natural tendency to please, to be liked, to be lovely. It exposes us to the potential pain of feeling rejection and failure.

Understand that nearly every aspect of your life (at work and at home) is negotiable, and that over a lifetime the cumulative results of asking or not asking for what you want can be dramatic. Being willing to ask can mean millions more dollars, more time to enjoy your life, less stress, stronger relationships, better health, and greater happiness.

ASK FOR WHAT YOU WANT

Start by asking the Universe for what you desire, but don't stop there. Ask your employer, your lover, your mechanic, and even your credit card company for what you want (money/promotion, support, discount, refund). I've asked for (and received) things I didn't expect to get . . . like getting into law school with no high school diploma or undergraduate education (albeit under probation). I still get mail asking for proof of my law degree because people think I'm lying. They assume it's impossible, and it was impossible—until I asked for it.

LEARN TO ASK FOR SMALL THINGS, TOO

Recently, I went out of town and missed my credit card payment by one day and was charged a late fee. I called the credit card company, explained that I was away, and asked them to remove the charge. They did. I made $35 in five minutes, and that's a pretty good rate! There is no ceiling on what someone can say "Yes" to. All you have to lose is the "No" you're guaranteed to get by not asking. So why not ask? Because it's uncomfortable? Unexpected? Ask anyway. Linda Babcock notes that the most successful way for a woman to negotiate is to be feminine, friendly, and kind, and demonstrate concern for others.

SAY "NO"

Learn how to say "No" to requests that make your life difficult. It's not rude or inappropriate, but rather an act of competent self-care. When you say "No," be clear and definitive. Don't hem and haw about it. You don't need to explain your reasons, even though most women feel they must. The simplest, most effective way to say "No" is to say it nicely once, and then be quiet. Learn to get comfortable with the silence in conversations. If you need to fill the space, silently say the alphabet or hum a tune in your head. It's okay.

NEVER MAKE PERSONAL LOANS

If you cannot give the money as a gift, do not lend it. Loans are usually made with the best intentions. The borrower is eager to pay the money back, and it feels good to help someone you love. Unfortunately, things often don't go as planned. In many cases, the borrower encounters additional challenges and cannot (or chooses not to) repay the loan. Relationships suffer and so does the financial welfare of the lender. Only loan money when you can give it away and feel good about it. If this is the case, make the loan without telling the borrower it's a gift. If it comes back to you, wonderful. If not, you will still have your peace of mind.

OWN YOUR PLACE IN CREATION

See yourself as an integral piece of the Universe, and recognize your responsibility and obligation to support abundance by joyously circulating resources—giving and receiving.

Remember Sara, who made an appearance at the beginning of this section? She found her courage and implemented everything we discussed. As a result, she retained all of her clients. One even mentioned that he wondered how she had managed to survive charging such low rates. Sara has rehired her assistant and is taking her first vacation in years. This experience prompted Sara to learn more about herself and explore the reasons why she limited herself financially for so long.

At some point, all women grapple with insecurity over their worthiness and value. It takes self-awareness and objectivity to overcome it. Your self-image, and how it shows up in outward expression, is always reflected back to you. Tend it wisely.

NOTE

1. For detailed examples and effective negotiation techniques, see Linda Babcock and Sara Laschever's *Women Don't Ask: The High Cost of Avoiding Negotiation—and Positive Strategies for Change* (New York: Bantam Dell, 2007)

35

MASCULINITY AS A TOOL

*Facing a challenge on the coliseum floor, the
Goddess wields staffs, shields, swords, and more.*

For women in careers perceived as masculine in nature (mana-
gerial, political, and corporate leadership), to be successful, you
must be able to plot a path through a mine field of conflicting
stereotypes and perspectives. Despite the advances made since the
women's movement, only three percent of Fortune 500 CEOs
are women. In general, women, especially feminine women,
are presumed to be less competitive, competent, and ambitious
than men. If you dream of reaching high levels of management
within an organization, you will have to master the qualities of
self-confidence and assertiveness. At the same time, you must
incorporate supportiveness and interpersonal sensitivity, or risk
being perceived as a bitch and miss out on promotions because
no one likes you. In essence, in certain environments, a woman
must act like a man to succeed, but she can also fail for not behaving like a woman.

In 2011, researchers from the George Mason School of Management and the Stanford Graduate School of Business reported
their findings that women who are capable of self-monitoring
(accurately assessing social situations and choosing appropriate
responses to those situations) are able to overcome the negative
backlash that women experience when they behave in a mas-

culine manner.[1] What amazed me the most was the finding that women who were highly skilled at self-monitoring received one and a half times more promotions than both their masculine male and feminine female counterparts. They received two times the promotions of feminine men, and three times more promotions than their masculine-acting, low self-monitoring female counterparts. A woman who knows when to apply masculinity, and when not to, will be more successful than any other type of corporate manager, even masculine men. The most fascinating aspect of these results is that the feminine ability to shape-shift—to know how to flow and what form to take—gives us the power to excel in organizations and even to surpass men.

You can consciously apply masculinity as a tool to advance your goals beyond the boardroom, too. Whatever the situation, let your intuition help you select the right tools to achieve your desires with the least effort. By choosing the tone of expression most likely to result in a desired outcome, you will be more successful than men and women who use only masculine or feminine expression.

Ella grew up believing a forceful, aggressive, dominant woman was a strong woman and that the only way to be powerful was to amplify her masculine energy. It took a massive upheaval to send her back to her feminine grace. Her husband was severely injured in an accident, and Ella became responsible for her family, businesses, and debts—for everything.

The loss of income and the addition of significant medical expenses placed tremendous stress on her finances. To make ends meet, she needed to sell a partnership interest she held in a property. By agreement, she had to sell it to the majority shareholder, or go through a complex process to gain the right to sell it to someone else. Ella didn't have the time, energy, or resources to find another buyer or fight the majority shareholder, yet she loathed the idea of selling to him. He was shrewd, aggressive, and manipulative in every area of his life. From a distance, she'd watched him operate for years. He loved winning, and the more he was able to force his opponent to relinquish, the greater his satisfaction. He was known to use his legal team to tie up a matter in endless convoluted legal confrontations as a tactic to wear down his opponent and get his way.

Ella was no pushover; she had an MBA and several years of complex negotiation experience. She was more than capable of aggressively holding her own at any level, but this time she just couldn't. She was reeling from the tragedy of her husband's disability. She knew the costs of handling the buyout "man-to-man" would be high. For months, she dreaded the confrontation and the losses she expected at the hands of the majority shareholder. She feared he would sense the emptiness in her conviction to fight, and pillage what was left. She wanted better for her family, but she didn't have the fortitude or finances to fight him.

Ella spent months conducting appraisals, coming up with a value she felt was fair, and agonizing over negotiation strategies. Her intuition told her there had to be more than one way to win. She came up with a plan foreign to anything she'd tried before. She decided to use a peaceful, submissive approach. It wasn't promising, but she knew a brute-force, lawyer-like strategy would certainly fail.

With her target price written on a business card and tucked into her purse, she pulled open the towering mahogany doors to the majority shareholder's offices. He wore the smug expression of a well-fed cat. She spoke to him calmly, from a centered place of stability and substance. Ella spoke directly to the human being she knew had to live somewhere inside him. When he brought up his own lawyers, appraisers, and valuation models, she reminded him that the two of them were quite capable of handling the matter without lawyers. She said her goal was to resolve everything quickly, fairly, and collaboratively. When he moved into his harsh business persona routine, Ella interrupted and asked, "Why fight? Only the lawyers will win, and we are better than that."

Repeatedly, Ella refused to walk the warpath and returned to peace. She stayed in her power and womanly strength. Finally, he thawed, and he made her an initial offer that was lower than her target price. Using the feminine power of connected communication, she presented her own valuation and reasoning, and calmly asked for what she wanted. He sat back in his chair and paused, regarding her for a moment before rocking forward to say, "Ella, you should work for me."

Within a week, the deal was done. Ella got the price she wanted without the pain, strain, and expense of battling lawyers. They both won.

I've used the same feminine intelligence to resolve many deals and disputes. I've learned that when you challenge a dominant masculine type to a fight, male or female, they'll give it to you.

As natural leaders, healers, and preservers of peace in the world, we have the power to orchestrate outcomes that benefit all parties. The key to success is to be able to accurately assess when to employ the forces of masculinity and when to rely on feminine grace.

NOTE

1. See Olivia A. Oneill and Charles A. O'Reilly III's paper "Reducing the backlash effect: Self-monitoring and women's promotions," in the *Journal of Occupational and Organizational Psychology*, vol 84, Issue 4: pp 825–832 (2011)

36

STARTING OR RETURNING TO WORK IN THE GODDESS'S PRIME

Free of the myths pervading young minds,
the workplace is a treasure chest for the
Goddess in her prime.

Whether by choice or necessity, many women start or return to professional careers in midlife—an age marking a new and potentially wondrous part of life. Our youth-worshipping culture fosters negative associations regarding this stage in life, but reasons abound to embrace this time when you can let go of all that does not serve you. You are born anew. Enjoy your second spring.

Women who've spent years giving everything to motherhood are the most qualified women in the world. They are wise, competent, resilient, responsible, and creative problem-solvers. Information on the latest technologies and procedures can be learned quickly. Competence takes years to develop. Women who have successfully nurtured children into adulthood possess a wellspring of strengths and can learn whatever information is required.

If you're starting a career in midlife, the single most important thing you can do is give value to your gifts, skills, and strengths. If the world is to see your worth, you must see it first. You may be feeling as though these words are intended for someone other than you. They aren't. I'm writing to all women.

You have tremendous gifts, strengths, and capacities. You've endured difficulties, potentially devastating ones, and you've thrived. If you've made it this far into this book, you are a feminine woman, and one of your strengths is fluidity. Like water, you can always find a channel to your destination. Nothing can stop you.

The challenge is to dump the negative messages you might have picked up about women in midlife and beyond. They aren't remotely true. Fortify yourself with inspiration. Learn the stories behind the successes of women who are enjoying wonderful careers. This is your time. For many women, it's their first opportunity to spend the bulk of their time taking care of their own needs and working for their own benefit. Believe in yourself and take daily steps toward your goals, regardless of what anyone says.

Leah married a wealthy businessman when she was 24 years old. Together, they had three children. Leah stayed home with the children; she was active in school functions, helped out on the kids' sports teams, managed the family finances, and helped her husband entertain business clients. Nearly 20 years into their marriage, the sands of her stable life began to shift. The children were in college, and their absence highlighted the fact that she and her husband lived separate lives. After a few months of counseling, Leah's marriage ended amicably.

After making the difficult transition from married to single woman, Leah was confronted with the need to earn her own money. Having no professional experience and feeling lost, she took the brave step of enrolling in a real estate course. Three months later, she earned a real estate license.

Thinking she had nothing more than textbook understanding of real estate and sales, she took her license into a Beverly Hills real estate agency and asked for a job. The agency's manager happened to be in a bind. There were no agents available to stay in the office and answer incoming sales calls, so he was forced to take the calls himself instead of handling his extraordinarily large workload. He asked Leah if she was willing to start immediately and handle the phones. Though she was terrified and wanted to bolt, Leah accepted. The manager handed her a book containing the office's current listings and left her all alone.

When the first phone call came in, Leah felt nauseated. She feared she had no idea how to sell real estate. She soon discovered that her ability to listen, care, and solve problems was all it took to sell a house. That day, she sold her first house and over time became one of the highest-earning agents in Beverly Hills.

Leah didn't listen to society, her friends, or her family's fears. She even had the good sense to blow off her divorce attorney's admonition to scale down her lifestyle to a level low enough to live on her alimony and accept that life is tough for divorcées.

In any economy or circumstance, someone is succeeding. It might as well be you. You don't need to concern yourself with how things will come together, just take consistent steps in the direction of your goals. You are more capable than you know, and the universe conspires to help those who help themselves.

PART V
RESURRECTING VENUS

37

THE AURORA

Farewell to the darkness, the heaviness is gone.
Today marks your renaissance, a new day, the dawn.

The aurora is the dawn. It's the moment you realize you are a unique incarnation of Venus. When you plant your feet firmly on the path to embodying your truest self, the aurora marks your renaissance. The veil between you and the Wild Divine dissolves, and a new, magnificent way of being emerges. It may excite you, bring you great relief, or feel too good to be true. You may mistakenly believe that you've discovered something new, but there is nothing new here. It's just that you've unearthed what resonates with you the most: your truest self.

If you love beauty, it's because beauty lives within you. If you love art, it's because you are creative. If you fawn over romance novels, it's because you're a passionate woman, no matter how you may deny her. If it wakes up your heart, a receptor for it must already exist within you. Your soul is drawn to the things that will help you unfold your most glorious expression. Give in. There is no greater success than to give up the little self, the ego, and shine the Goddess forth. Surrender to the will of the Creator, and recognize the magnificence incarnated as you. This is the path to heaven here on earth. As the poet Rumi so rightly noted, "What you seek is seeking you." It's a divine conspiracy.

We do not live in an accidental universe, the result of some cosmic chaos that haphazardly managed to pile up and produce life. No. An infinite organizing intelligence with intentions and capacities far beyond our comprehension, call it what you will—God, Spirit, Creation, Love, Energy, Light—this Power is the sum total of all existence. We cannot fully know the divine mind, but we can connect with it enough to heal our hearts, banish fear, and live as a free and joyful expression of it.

The whispers of God's heart are written all over creation. Azure oceans, emerald forests, watercolor sunsets, and moonlit meadows reveal our Creator's love of beauty. The abundance of air, the feast of foods, pristine waters, and plentiful materials on earth tell us that we are intended to thrive. Our instinct from birth to seek comfort, warmth, and physical contact demonstrates the divine intent that intimacy, love, affection, and connection be fundamental in our lives. The moments, people, places, and things with the power to take our breath away convey the Infinite's desire to awe and inspire us. Though tragedy, disaster, and destruction may seem incongruous, pain (our pain or another's) is a guiding mechanism to tell us we've fallen off track or to teach us compassion.

Disaster and destruction may appear before our human eyes, yet at every moment divine harmony is the governing force of the universe. Our Creator's most indelible stroke across humanity is our drive to seek happiness. Reduced to its purest form, this is the drive to seek Spirit, the soul's urge to come home. But when the ego takes hold of the human mind, it tricks us into believing that happiness can be found in stuff and status. Like a charming predator, it mesmerizes us, dangling a plastic nirvana before our hungry eyes. Then it devours us alive.

Heaven on earth is born of the realization that we are at one with the Infinite, and every appearance of separation is always and only an illusion. We were made in, by, and for love. When we wake to this truth, we see the Divine everywhere. Even a single flower reveals the love, beauty, and majesty of life, when quietly asked to tell its secrets.

In one exquisite moment, the Divine focused entirely on creating the first and the last incarnation of a unique being: you. If you believed that you were a one-of-a kind, custom creation made by the greatest artist of all time, how would you live? Would you honor your Creator and live boldly utilizing all the gifts bestowed upon you, or would you resist, muddling around until your time was up?

Many of us were taught to believe that a white, moody, male God power sits somewhere in the sky watching us. We are asked to believe that an omnipotent, omniscient, omnipresent God created all people, but only acknowledges those who read the right books, pray the proper prayers, believe a certain tenet, or follow specific rituals. The idea that any child will die and not return to the Divine because she didn't follow the right dogma is plausible only to those who put religion before God. Fear silences the loving heart.

Turn to love, live it in all you do, and let it guide your journey. Surrender the rules, the ways, and the modes mankind invented to control the free expression of people, specifically women. Set yourself free to follow the path Spirit created in you. The Divine is and always has been for you, never away from you, and never against you. The deep desires of your heart are mandates from the great Creator calling you to live, to love, and to express the Divine as you.

"Thy will be done" is a wonderful prayer to pray if you want to live in glorious expansion. God's will and the deepest desires of your heart are mirrors of each other.

"The Lord is my Shepherd; I shall not want" (Psalms 23:1) is a confirmation of the abundance that is already free-flowing and available. An infinite river of supply is always flowing around you. Open to receive it. Let prosperity, ease, and satisfaction be part of your life.

"I do nothing on my own, the Infinite Spirit does the work" is the antidote for the ego's belief that you are alone in the face of fear, intimidation, or doubt. The ego would have you believe that you are superior or inferior, the master or the slave. Not so. You are a divine child of God. At every moment, guidance, abundance, and oneness are present, available, and intended for you.

Your work is to discover and maintain your conscious awareness of and contact with the Divine. When you live at this level of connection, all things are possible. Let it be so.

38

YOU, THE CHOSEN ONE

Out of eternity,
your name was called to receive life,
a gift more precious than all.

Imprisoned within the walls of unhealthy competition, criticism, self-doubt, and insecurity, countless women languish, waiting for some illustrious person, authority, or event to choose them. We are "Sleeping Beauties" lying unconscious as thorns grow over our lives. If only our "prince" would come and set us free. When we get the job, receive the promotion, win the award, get noticed, or finally get him to propose, it will prove to *us* and the world that we are valuable, worthy, and enough. Behind the walls of our illusory prison, we wait—hoping that happiness is on the other side and that we will be picked by whatever aim or person we've chosen to be our prince.

Who must select you? What must you achieve before you finally feel good enough, successful, or complete? The answer is no one and nothing. You've already been chosen for the most significant honor of all: life. The Infinite gave you life.

Buddhists liken the chances of having a human incarnation to the chances of an ox's yoke floating on an ocean as large as the earth, and a blind turtle lifting his head out of the water once in 100 years and poking his head through the yoke. It's precious, rare, coveted, and on purpose. You are here by divine design. You aren't a mistake; Spirit doesn't make mistakes. The Creator loves you so much that you were given a gift more valuable than any worldly thing. Can you think of a title, role, status, achievement, or award that transcends the exaltation that has been bestowed upon you? You were chosen for life, and there is nothing greater.

It's well past time that women dissolve the prison of illusions and release the disabling notion that someone or something must choose us before we can be, do, and have what we want. We are and always have been enough. Perish any thought to the contrary.

Since Claire was a child, she's dreamed of being an actress. Growing up in Iowa, she studied drama in high school and attended one of the country's leading thespian academies. Her teachers told her she was talented and would be an on-screen sensation. After graduation, Claire moved to Los Angeles, had pictures taken, and sent them to hundreds of local agents and casting directors. Several called to acknowledge they'd received her submission, but they weren't interested. The majority never called. Determined to find a way in, Claire finagled access to the casting notices (daily want ads sent to agents), and she began showing up at auditions without an agent. One year later, she still had no agent, no union affiliation (a must have), and no work. Claire interpreted the lack of interest as a statement of her unworthiness, inferiority, and unattractiveness. She became depressed, started staying out late with friends at bars, and missing the morning casting notices. Her acting dreams sat like moaning children in her belly and she was unable to feed or console them.

I met Claire just as she was contemplating moving back to Iowa. When she described her passion to act, it was apparent that she really loved the craft. It wasn't about fame, money, adoration, or ego gratification. For her, it was art.

"So what's the hold-up?" I asked. "If you want to be an actress, why aren't you acting?"

Claire shot me a quizzical look, wondering if I was serious. When she realized I was, she explained that no one would give her a chance; no one would choose her.

"Choose yourself," I interrupted, because it was obvious that Claire had bought into the rules, the way things are "supposed" to happen. She was doing what 99.9 percent of people do: follow the expected path and play by the rules.

"Claire, if you want to be an actress, act," I said. "Find a way to make it happen and share it with the world. Stop following the rules. Make new rules that favor you. We are blessed to live in a time when communication is easier than ever before. With a camera, even a mobile phone camera, and access to a computer, you can produce, air, and promote your own show. If it's good—and you'll have to do the work to make it better than great—people will share it, and you'll be amazed at what happens. Anything is possible."

Claire took my advice and recruited the best actresses and actors she'd met in her classes. Together, they created a weekly webisode and promoted it online. The show was rough at first, but the actors were talented, hardworking, and nimble. Each week, they tweaked the format and content until the show became fun to watch. A small niche of Internet devotees developed, and soon Claire was doing what she had always wanted, acting. Something else happened, too; casting directors began calling her for auditions. Within three months of finding the right mix of actors and a storyline, Claire had signed with an agent, booked two parts, and joined the actors' union. Soon after that, she became a regular on a popular TV series.

Instead of waiting to be picked, Claire made her own work, and the barriers between her and her goal collapsed. Claire is no more worthy today than she was when she started. All she did was free herself from illusion and the expectations of others, and make up her own rules.

Right now, believe you are enough. You already are chosen. Live from this truth.

39

YOUR BIRTHRIGHTS

A woman requires no permission
to sip the wine of her own vineyard.

Over the course of my coaching and blogging career, I've encountered a troublesome, but consistent dynamic with clients and readers. It occurs with even the most educated and powerful women. Here's how it goes: A woman comes to me seeking help in finding her right work, love, or sense of self. We spend time figuring out what she wants most and—usually just as we approach the threshold of taking action toward her most elusive dreams—the amazing woman before me, whether a doctor, TV producer, lawyer, or homemaker, transforms into a wide-eyed, uncomfortable little girl.

Vulnerable and insecure, her uncertain eyes bore into me. I know what she needs. I know that I can't give it to her, and I feel frustrated that as far as women have come, we still do not own our power. At the same time, I want to hold her close, soothe and protect her, and tell her I love her and have the power to help her. So I pretend that I have the power and authority to give her what she needs. I give her permission. When she goes out into the world and does what she believes I gave her permission to do,

I explain that I had nothing to do with it. I am a naked emperor. I've never had the power to change anyone. *Change is an inside job.*

After years of practice, I've accepted that sometimes women do require the appearance of permission from someone outside themselves, someone they admire and trust. It's the only way to overwrite the limitations placed on them by some other naked emperor, someone who had access to their heart, usually a parent or love interest. Telling the lost little girl within that no one has any power over her unless she agrees to it, or that everything she believes is only an idea she agreed to accept, doesn't help her. She can't own this. She still needs permission.

Interestingly, when asked whether other women are entitled to live and enjoy the benefits of the same birthrights, every single woman pipes up with a wholehearted "Yes." We will champion the rights of another woman without hesitation, but often we won't show up for ourselves.

You are entitled to know and live by the following list of rights, just by the very fact that you exist. These rights are yours. You don't need to deserve, earn, struggle, or fight to have them. They belong to you. If any part of you needs permission to accept any of these rights, I'm here to give it to you. It's my hope that you will join me in giving permission to yourself, your children, and all women. As you read over the list, you may feel that you already know or utilize a certain right. I encourage you to take a close look at your life and explore new ways of expressing that right. Every birthright offers endless opportunities for joyful expression, and once you master one level of expression, another awaits.

YOUR BIRTHRIGHTS

You have the right and my permission to:

BE JOYFUL

Joy is your birthright. It's not something you need to earn or deserve. Cultivate joy by reminding yourself that you are one with the Divine. Never alone, you are always loved, always entitled to God's grace. Living with joy will transform your entire life, because the state of your consciousness influences what you attract, notice, and respond to. Make joy your basic state of being. It's your right.

KNOW YOU ARE ENOUGH

The fear of not being enough sabotages women at every level of success and in every area of life. Many of us move through life in a haze of thinking, *What if I'm not enough?* It shakes our confidence in key moments, causes us to self-sabotage our own success; sometimes, it completely paralyzes us. In any case, it drains our energy and diverts us from reaching our dreams. Develop your own inner sunbeam to burn off the haze of "not enough." Familiarize yourself with women who have what you want or do what you want to do. If you look closely, you'll discover things about them that could have stopped them from trying to reach their goals; often, these are the very things you use to hold yourself back. These women aren't lucky, they're wise. They know that being enough is a choice. Choose to believe you are enough. Do it right now.

CELEBRATE YOUR BEAUTY

You have the right and my permission to be beautiful and to shine that beauty out to the world. The Temple of Venus is a miraculous vessel of creation that perplexes and mystifies even the most brilliant minds. Inherently beautiful in its diverse appearances, the treasure we inhabit is more priceless than any material luxury. The Bentley you may dream of one day possessing is a tractor next to your empyrean form. All of humankind has entered the world through the magnificence of this exquisite creation. Any woman blessed with the clarity to see the opulent luxury, artistic mastery, and creative blessing of the female structure, will stand in awestruck gratitude. Our work is never to become beautiful; it's to recognize that we already *are* beautiful. To enhance your beauty is an inside job, to be performed primarily for your pleasure and satisfaction. Though romantic partners are likely to scale a thorn-covered wall just to glimpse your grace, see them as a side benefit, not a primary motivation. Cultivate your beauty for you. You deserve to be healthy, radiant, and delighted with yourself. Begin with the essence of beauty: the love in your heart. Develop a self-love practice. Remember, love is a verb, something you do. Show yourself how much you love yourself. Praise, comfort, encourage, and believe in you. Lavish your body with nutritious foods and enjoyable exercise. Meditate. Acknowledge each time you do something loving for yourself. To practice self-love cultivates true beauty, the kind that shines through your eyes and from your heart. It also improves your health, physical appearance, and energy levels. Even women who defy all classic standards of beauty become extraordinarily, irresistibly magnetic and beautiful when they practice self-love.

BE SELFISH

As girls, we were conditioned to behave in ways that pleased others. Children whom society perceives as "good" receive more positive attention and love than children who resist conformity. When we share, give, and compromise, people are nicer to us. As adults, many women, in an effort to please, agree to things they don't really want. We give our time, money, attention, and effort to things that don't serve us out of guilt or a sense of obligation. We do what we believe we should and feel uncomfortable when we do what we really want. You cannot fulfill your desires through obedience and seeking outside approval. To achieve your dreams, you must become selfish. You were probably taught to believe that selfishness is wrong or makes you insensitive to others, but it doesn't. When a woman who values love, kindness, and connection behaves selfishly, she will become more loving and kind. The more you take care of yourself, the greater ability you'll have to care for the people and causes that mean the most to you. This form of selfishness, taking care of yourself, magnifies your essence. By selfishly following your heart, you open the channel for your greatest expression. Your path to success is accelerated, because you will act with endurance, stamina, and devotion. You will also become a magnet and model for other women. Put your health, happiness, success, and welfare above the needs of others, and you will have more of everything to give. Embrace being selfish. One vital exception: Mothers with minor children must include their children in their definition of self. Our highest concern must be the best interests of our children, even if this entails periods and acts of self-sacrifice.

LIVE YOUR WAY

I used to keep a quote on my office wall from a journalist named Christopher Morley that said, "There is only one success—to be able to spend your life in your own way." I hid it behind my home office's door so when my (then) husband opened the door, he wouldn't see it. I knew the quote was true, but I felt selfish for believing it. A part of me believed I was wrong unless I did what the world and my peers expected, meaning spend the holidays at my in-laws', send Christmas cards, play golf, and join all the mothers' clubs at school. The thing is, I prefer being home on holidays; I only like to send cards when I'm moved to write something heartfelt; I despise golf; and I have a visceral urge to flee when surrounded by "mommy talk" about potties, time-outs, and tantrums. Yet I spent many frustrated years living up to other people's expectations. It took the tragedy of my husband's illness to shake me awake to the realization that *this is it*. Life is short and unpredictable. How long can you wait to live life *your* way? Not a single second. Take a giant marker and line out everything on your list of "to do's" that aren't yours. You don't have to marry, be heterosexual, have children, get a certain education, go where you don't want to go, live a particular way, follow a religion, or do anything else that breaks your spirit. If you choose to do something you don't really want to do, be sure you have a monumental reason. You may choose it for someone else's benefit. That's wonderful, if giving to another person makes you feel fulfillment, love, and happiness. If you give with an edge of resentment, stop it. You aren't helping anyone unless you choose to live your life your way.

ENJOY SUCCESS, ABUNDANCE, AND HAPPINESS

A surprisingly large number of women feel guilty or embarrassed by their good fortune. They feel that somehow it isn't fair for them to have so much good in their lives while others have so little. Imagine a world where no one enjoyed life. It would be hell. You don't need to gloat or lose your humility to own the greatness in your life. Your success is a call for celebration and a possible source of inspiration for others. Consider yourself a pathlighter and point others in the direction of greatness. Give back and encourage them. If you're just starting on the path toward success, know that whatever your heart desires, whatever makes you feel fully alive, you have the right to go after it. Go boldly and receive without apology. What you accept for yourself, you accept for all women.

THINK FOR YOURSELF
AND TRUST YOUR INTUITION

Question what you read, hear, and observe, no matter the source. If it doesn't feel right to you, don't be afraid to throw it out. Apply this to all information and teachings, including mine. Trust your inner guidance and think for yourself. Don't allow fear of being wrong, making a mistake, or offending someone cause you to ignore your intuition. You can use your intuition to help you navigate every situation. Practice feeling the energy in your core—the place two inches above your navel. Innate wisdom and exquisite guidance emanate from here. Learn to recognize it. Check your conclusions against logic and available resources, but never suppress, deny, or abandon what you know for sure.

REMOVE YOURSELF
FROM UNWANTED SITUATIONS

More than a right, this is really an obligation. You are responsible for your (and your children's) care and welfare. When you find yourself in an unwanted or harmful situation, it's your duty to take yourself out of it. The Internet brings a whole new aspect to consider when upholding this idea. Recently I participated in an online discussion about relationships. In the beginning, the exchanges were thoughtful and interesting. In time, however, they became vulgar, sexually explicit, and offensive. At first, I responded by ignoring the graphic language and focusing on my own views. When I left the exchange, I felt sullied, as though I had spent an evening in a seedy bar surrounded by callous heathens. Later I mentioned my experience to a close male friend, and he pointed out that were the same conversation to have occurred in person, I'd have removed myself from the situation at the first whisper of inappropriateness and precluded any further contact. Why would I tolerate anything different online? He was right. I am responsible for the people and experiences I allow in my life. If I want to be surrounded by interesting people who want to learn and grow in respectful ways, then I must nurture these relationships and not engage with people who darken my experience. They are entitled to live the life they choose, but I don't have to be affected by it. I sent a note to the discussion leader explaining that I was leaving the group and wished him well. I felt relieved. The moment you become aware of your power to put an end to what does not serve you is the moment you realign with your true self.

CHOOSE PEACE

Chaos happens. Relationships spin out of control, we lose someone or something dear, our bodies get sick, and finances unravel. Things fall apart, and it can be disorienting. We may believe we are victims and lose precious years riding the turmoil. Being chaotic is not a solution to chaos; being peaceful is. True power emerges out of emotional and mental stillness. Chaos needs fuel. It feeds on fear and anger. Starve it. Poison it with gratitude and love for what remains. If you're in the throes of a storm, know that right now you can take control of the only thing you've ever had control over, *you*. You can count on yourself. You are a powerful being who can choose stillness and peace, even now. This is a practice that takes work—everything worthwhile does. From a place of stillness, helpful perspectives, options, and solutions will emerge. You can come to know that you are bigger than any challenge you face. In the midst of chaos, you have the right to choose peace.

BE LOVED JUST THE WAY YOU ARE

You are worthy and deserving of love at this very moment. You have nothing to do or become to receive the fullness of the love that exists for you right now. Sometimes it helps to remember that love is an eternal, pervasive energy. It never fails or dies. Every loving thought about you stays with you always. In every moment, you are loved. Do not believe that you require the love of any particular person. If you can feel love in your heart, you have access to all the love in the universe. Show yourself love by being kind, compassionate, and lovingly disciplined. When you practice self-love, others will be drawn to you. Through the realization that you already *are* love, new experiences of love will be born.

40

SURRENDER VICTIMHOOD

In never allowing another credit for her pain,
the Goddess ensures power over her life and gain.

[NOTE: Please understand that the "victims" I speak of in this section are not children, crime victims, or victims of abuse. If you are a crime or abuse victim, or you know someone who is, please seek professional help and support.]

Victimhood is one of the greatest impediments to successful living. It's the state of believing that someone or something else is responsible for the content, quality, or experience of your life. You *can* take empowered responsibility for yourself and your experience, and create a life you love and one that serves you.

You might believe that you don't feel or behave like a victim, and, therefore, this doesn't apply to you. In fact, it's often easier to see victim behavior in others than it is to see it in our own thoughts and actions. At some point, everyone has felt like a victim, and even the most empowered person may still have moments of victim-like thinking from time to time. I've yet to meet anyone who can't benefit from taking a look at their victim-like tendencies. Open your mind and get curious about yourself. You have nothing to lose and everything to gain.

Let's take a look at the qualities of people who believe they are victims. Often, they:

- React to outside events and people instead of proactively creating their desires

- Lack direction—like feathers in the wind, they land where they land

- Believe that God, the government, their spouse, or their parents are in control of their life

- Blame others for their circumstances—blame is the victim's trademark

- Feel helpless and stuck

- Feel separate from their Creator

- Dwell on past events that appear to have "stolen" or prevented their good or harmed them, and

- See the world as a dangerous and scary place.

Victims live in constant fear. Always bracing for the next bad thing to happen, they have no plan or direction. Since they are always busy and exhausted handling the next crisis, they mistakenly believe that they are productive. Deep inside, they don't really expect to attain their dreams, and they can rapidly list the people, events, and conditions responsible.

The pay-off for the victim is that they never have to admit failure. If everything is outside of their influence, they are beyond blame. The victim is never responsible for any negative outcome. They cannot lose the game because they never suit up to play. Though this may appear to be a shortcut to an easier life, victims suffer hopelessness, a fate worse than failure. In avoiding the risks of failure and loss, they squash all potential for success. They can never win.

Though it may seem brutal to admit, you are responsible for the good and bad in your life. All of it. Every decision you make, every perception you hold, and every action you take or refrain from taking becomes a strand in the fabric of your life. Even the passive act of allowing others to make decisions for you is your responsibility. When you emerge from a bad relationship, business deal, or situation, whatever occurred is your responsibility, too.

Women often balk at this idea and offer detailed factual analyses of why it isn't true; but ultimately there is always a point of action, or passive inaction, on the part of the "victim" without which the aggravating circumstance could not have occurred. The value in realizing this and accepting responsibility for your part is not to shift blame to you and make you feel horrible. On the contrary, taking responsibility for every aspect of your life, the positive and the negative, puts you in control of it. If you are the one accountable for the conditions and circumstances of your life, then you are the one who can change them. This is where a fulfilling life begins.

Recently, I made a comment online about the empowering effects of taking responsibility for your own life. A woman responded saying she disagreed. She went on to explain that feelings of inadequacy and repeated failures beyond her control made it impossible for her to get out of being stuck. Here's how I responded:

"You're living the heroine's struggle. The heroine says 'I will create my dreams,' but soon, all manner of challenges arise. Darkness swirls, and it seems as though failure is certain. Yet she perseveres. She digs deeper, looks for new methods, and continues her dogged pursuit. She falls often, but she only becomes a failure if she refuses to get back up. So long as she perseveres, success follows. Every success story goes this way. This is what we pay to watch in theaters. It's what we admire in others. You may not be able to control each encounter, event, or outcome in your life, but you can *always* control your perception and reaction to it. For the person who chooses to respond powerfully, success is inevitable. Please know this is true. Don't give up. Try new things, talk to new people, change your view, and believe in yourself. There is no question that a solution exists for you. *No question.* You just need to receive or discover it."

To heal the victim mind requires that you consciously adopt a new, empowered perspective and eliminate old patterns. Imagine gradually pouring fresh, clean water into a cup of clouded water. At some point, the cup will overflow, and if you keep pouring in clean water, soon the cup will hold only clear water. Clearing ourselves of victim consciousness is a similar process. The cloudy water represents victim-like thinking. By consistently choosing to apply healthy, self-loving, empowered thoughts and practices, you can change your state of mind and your life.

Every thought is an affirmation, and we are thinking nearly all of the time. Instead of affirming by default, choose the affirmations that create your life. Choose one or more of the following affirmations, or create one that feels good to you. A well-chosen affirmation causes a shift in you the first few times you say it.

- I am the most powerful person in my life.
- I can be what I choose to be.
- Nothing real stands between my good and me.
- I release all ideas of victimhood and go free.
- I take responsibility for every event and circumstance in my life.
- I live in a friendly Universe and life is on my side.
- I know my heart's desires and take daily action toward them.

- ❋ The "how" will reveal itself at the perfect moment.
- ❋ The size of a problem means nothing to the Infinite. Anything is possible for me.
- ❋ The Universe conspires to help me when I help myself.
- ❋ I release and forgive everyone. It is done. I go free.

For the next three weeks, which is the time it takes to build a new habit, repeat your affirmation(s), silently and aloud, often. Think about what they mean. Make them the first and last thought of the day. Reread this section; challenge and reflect on it. Search for examples of your victim-like behaviors. Go deep. Do not blame yourself when you catch yourself in victimhood. Remember, this is the victim's trademark. Assume your rightful position as the leader of your life.

41

FORGIVENESS IS FREEDOM

The prisons we build for others are the ones we will rot in.

[NOTE: This writing on forgiveness is not intended for people who are in the throes of a crisis. Neither is it intended to rationalize the continued tolerance of intolerable situations. If you are currently suffering from emotional upheaval, take the well-deserved and brave step of seeking professional/spiritual/religious help. Forgiveness intersects with the path of healing, but until you've begun to heal, it can be too much, too soon. In situations like these, try to hold a place of possibility and desire for the ability to forgive in the future.]

Forgiveness is the most vital and most misunderstood step in creating the life we dream of living. Due to widespread misconceptions about what forgiveness is and what it is not, the subject can trigger great resistance in even the most tenderhearted people. However, once understood, forgiveness will free your heart, soothe your spirit, and change the trajectory of your entire life.

As we go through life we cannot help but feel negative emotions from some interactions. Whether the upset is directed at a rude store clerk or someone who's caused us deep anguish, we often hold on to the memory and the resulting feelings and emotions. Most people are unaware of the damaging impact on their lives. Holding on to resentment, anger, jealousy, wounds of rejection, and other negative emotions can influence and shape every new interaction. For example, if you've had an unfaithful partner in the past—and you're holding on to that pain when you meet a new love—the very mistrust and hurt you want to avoid will color your behavior and bring suspicion into your new relationship. Similarly, if you've had a falling out with a family member and you are determined to have a better relationship, but you're still sore about the past, you will unconsciously infuse your present experience with poison from the past. Another example: Perhaps you're determined to start anew and become the greatest expression of you possible, but you're defensive. You've decided that you are not going to let anyone take advantage of you this time. Holding this thought makes you a magnet for people intent on taking advantage of others, including you.

Whatever you have not forgiven will continue to show up in your life. All of the negative emotions you carry forward act as a smoky haze clouding your perceptions, feelings, creativity, and motivations. When more negative experiences happen, and they will, the weight of the negativity grows. Lugging it all around with you is debilitating and harms every aspect of your life. In extreme situations, bitterness and cynicism become the dominant emotional states. Isolation and loneliness follow, because no one wants to keep company with a miserable person. Non-forgiveness turns you into a victim, because when you hold someone or something else responsible for your emotional state, you give away control of your feelings. The way you feel about yourself, others, and life shapes every action you take.

It's important to know what healthy forgiveness means. Forgiveness is the release of persistent negative thoughts and feelings that you harbor about yourself, someone else, or past events. It's not the acceptance of continued bad behavior. You are responsible for your personal care and safety, both emotional and physical. When someone harms you, they have demonstrated who they are, so believe them. Thinking they are different than their poor behavior is *your* poor judgment. Regardless of how many times the bad thing actually occurs, the first time it's their fault. If it happens again, and you could have left or avoided the situation, you share in the responsibility. Granted, there are exceptions (for example, stalkers and random or other unavoidable encounters), and sometimes people do change, but if the promised "change" is spurred by being caught cheating, lying, or committing some other harm, beware. The chances are high that the behavior or action will be repeated.

Sometimes, people are unwilling to forgive because they believe that the other person doesn't deserve their forgiveness. This thinking is flawed. No one suffers from your non-forgiveness more than you. You may think you shackle another in chains of non-forgiveness, but you bind only yourself. It's not about the offending person. It's all, and only, about you. Forgiveness benefits the forgiver.

The realization that unwillingness to forgive only compounds pain or upset is enough to motivate most people to let go. The next question is, "How do I forgive?" Here's what works for me:

I begin with the understanding that by holding on to non-forgiveness, I am harming myself, and by letting go of heavy negative thoughts and grudges, I free up space for new experiences of love, inspiration, success, connectedness, health, and power. I remind myself that forgiveness unties the chains that hold me hostage and prevent me from moving on. I acknowledge that I cannot take the actions of others personally. I know that I am not the real cause of their behavior, and that anyone who triggered their fear or upset the way I did would have received the same treatment. I remind myself that blame is the victim's trademark, and I refuse to subsist in victimhood. Beyond empowering myself, I know that forgiveness improves my health, relationships, and moment-to-moment well-being. I ask for help. I ask the power responsible for making my heart beat to take the burden from me. I "turn it over" to Spirit and give thanks that I am free. I reflect on the truth I've chosen to live my life by: Love is the most powerful force in existence and I am one with it. I cannot hold on to non-forgiveness and uphold my commitment to love myself. If the feelings are intense, I might write everything I have to say, unedited, unrestrained, and unfiltered, and when I can't come up with anything else, I (safely) burn the writings. Sometimes, I light a candle and send every unforgiving thought away in its flame. There may be ways that work better for you. I encourage you to seek them. How you forgive is not important, only that you do it. Only your freedom matters.

Often the person who needs forgiveness the most is you. In every situation, you've done the best you could with what you knew. Replace regret with gratitude for the lesson learned. Resolve to apply the wisdom you've gained and forgive yourself for all the ways you've disappointed yourself or others. You cannot create something positive using the negativity of yesterday. Forgive yourself and let go. Do this first and frequently. When the baggage and barriers of non-forgiveness are lifted, new and wonderful people and experiences will take their place. You deserve this.

42

BREAK OUT OF FITTING IN

A Goddess conforms solely to the dictates of her heart.

We are all conditioned to fit in. From the time of our birth, society, the media, our families, and our communities lay down edicts deep into our belief systems. We are complicit in our own domestication because we desire approval. It all happens effortlessly and automatically. By the time we reach the age of "independence," we are thoroughly programmed with the dominant beliefs, perspectives, and views of those around us.

You cannot create a deeply fulfilling life and conform to the expectations of others, too. The faster you let go of the desire to fit in and be liked, the sooner your magnificent life will unfold. To live in genuine self-governed freedom, examine and reconsider your most basic beliefs and assumptions. Often the beliefs you held as a young child are more consistent with your authentic truth than the ones you hold now. Return to your truth. Let go of what is in conflict with your most empowered state. Choose beliefs that resonate with you, not those that your friends, family, and community think are best for you. Abandon all life paths that others conditioned you to pursue. This is your life, and you will live every single moment of it with yourself. Only you know what's best for you.

If you have been unable to make progress toward a desired goal, look deeply into the programming you have about your success. For one woman, the idea of having several million dollars feels natural, freeing, and exciting. For another, it seems indulgent, selfish, and uncomfortable. The woman who harbors negative associations with wealth will unconsciously act in ways to prevent wealth from appearing in her life. From a universal perspective, both women are equally entitled to wealth or poverty. It's only belief that makes one woman attract wealth while another repels it.

What beliefs are ingrained in your programming? How are they helping or hindering your life? Read the following statements and notice your immediate reactions:

- The world is a safe place to experience all the things I enjoy.
- I can overcome whatever challenges arise in my life.
- I deserve to be wealthy.
- I shouldn't leave an unhappy marriage.
- I should feel happy all the time, or something is wrong.
- No one can be single and happy for a long time.
- Financial or career success after age 65 is unlikely.
- Nice people finish last; only the sharks get ahead.
- Settling for the safety of mediocrity is better than risking everything for a dream.
- Forgiveness is synonymous with weakness.
- Women are better mothers than they are executives.
- I have to fight hard and compete ruthlessly to succeed.

- There aren't many single, attractive, healthy, employed, generous, and available men out there.
- People over 50 can't be sexy and attractive.
- It's selfish to spend too much time or money on myself.
- I have to put up with bad or even abusive behavior from my family because we are related.
- Some people are just lucky.

Your reactions to the statements above reveal the underlying beliefs that create your life right now. No statement is inherently true, but they become true for those who believe them. If your beliefs do not reflect who you really are and the life you want to live, begin to release and replace your beliefs with empowering ideas that feel good. Pay no attention to the odds of success or what's common in the world. Determine to cut out a fresh path and witness the impossible as it unfolds. The first step is to become aware of what you'd like to change.

Get comfortable with the idea of being different from the people closest to you and the rest of the world. Release any need to fit in. Practice thinking for yourself in every situation. Question your preexisting beliefs and automatic reactions. When you find yourself in a situation that doesn't feel right to you, listen to your intuition. Fiercely honor your deepest feelings and inner knowing. After careful exploration and consideration, you may decide to retain a preexisting belief. That's fine. The important thing is to exercise your freedom and power to consciously choose the beliefs that reflect the greatest expression of you.

Be sure to be leery of things you feel that you "should" do. "Shoulds" are a snapping red flag. Beyond taking excellent care of yourself and your children, there is nothing else you *should* do.

You may choose it, but don't do a thing just because you think it's expected. Cut every cord to "should" and replace it with "could." Look within to decide whether something you formerly felt you should do serves your good. If it doesn't, determine whether there is a healthy reason to continue. Maybe the action benefits someone you care about, or serves others in a way that is worthwhile to you. However, under no circumstance is it okay to do something solely to avoid feelings of guilt. Going against yourself lowers self-trust. Heart-darkening beasts and guilty acts serve no one; they accumulate toxic levels of resentment inside of us until we erupt and spew venom on those we love. Everyone suffers. Be clear about what you are willing to do, and do no more.

After many years of practicing conscious thinking and choosing my own beliefs, I live by one fail-proof rule: Follow the light in your heart *wherever* it takes you. I am no longer bound by society's edicts. I feel more secure in myself than at any other time in my life. I live in the glorious freedom of being in harmony with my true self. You will not hurt anyone by being yourself and choosing what is best for you. Love does no harm. Trust this. Color your world with your own chosen hues. Give yourself this gift.

43

EMBRACE
A FRIENDLY UNIVERSE

In the Garden of the Goddess there is only plenty.

We do not live in a world created by random chance and populated with insignificant beings graced with the dumb luck of being alive. Far from it. We live in an ordered universe with a harmonizing mechanism that matches the dominant tone of our being. The law of attraction, a concept that has gained much popularity in recent years, has caused much confusion and misunderstanding about how to bring dreams to life. Rather than being a cosmic vending machine that spews out whatever we hold in our thoughts, the law of attraction is an energetic system of confirmation, multiplying, and returning to us the predominant vibrational energy we genuinely emanate from deep within. The vibration we emit is a result of our innermost thoughts, beliefs, and feelings. This vibration lines up with like vibrations in the universe, and energetically matched people, opportunities, and situations result.

To grasp the concept of vibrational energy with more clarity, think about the feeling tones of the different places you've visited. Hospitals, temples, preschools, and prisons have palpable frequencies of energy that reflect the vibration of what occurs most in each location. The experience of your life is a reflection of the dominant energies you emanate. It's no coincidence that an angry person commonly encounters upsetting people and situations. Similarly, most of us know at least one woman who is so immersed in low self-esteem and worthlessness that she can walk into a crowded room and end up going home with the only abusive and emotionally unavailable guy in the place. There are also those who seem to be the luckiest women alive. They move through the world easily, and enjoy great relationships, financial abundance, health, and freedom. They are literally a joy to be around because they spend their life vibrating from a consciousness of harmony and love. The full spectrum of energetic vibrations is always available to us, and whether by intention or default, we are always connected to a full range of frequencies. No one is predestined for or locked into a specific energy. Mastery of the conditions in our lives is born from cultivating a state of consciousness that emits the energy we wish to have reflected back to us.

Many women don't realize their power to set the tone and trajectory of their lives. Instead, they operate in reaction to the results of their unguided states of consciousness, fears, worries, and hindering beliefs. Your power as the queen of your life is to take responsibility for your predominant energetic state. As a human being, it's natural and inevitable for your feeling tone to change frequently. Maintaining a strong intention to spend most of your life in a state of receptive positivity will support you in cultivating the consciousness you want. The energy you align yourself with will become the dominant influence in your "Queendom."

Most women say they desire one thing—to be happy. Many believe that a certain item, person, or status will give them the happiness they crave. This is an erroneous assumption. If you were certain that money would make you happy, and you won the lottery but lost your sight, you would not be happy. No thing, person, or experience can give you enduring happiness. However, it's entirely possible to live from and multiply a state of deep joy, love, and abundance in your life. These are ever-present energies awaiting your alignment. Of them, love is the most powerful.

A few years ago, the movie *The Secret* swept the world with its promise of material gain through single-pointed mental and emotional determination. It was described as a manifestation process that went something like this: (1) name it; (2) unwaveringly claim it; and (3) watch it appear (with "it" being the object of your desire). I can't count the number of people I know who sat on their couches claiming cars, homes, and fame. They are more broke now than they were before. They lost precious time and endured much sadness when their wish list didn't manifest. When asked what they believe went wrong, they blame themselves for not being "faithful" or "focused" enough. Material items do not have a specific vibrational frequency. Money is a neutral energy. You can spend it on poison or paradise. You must align your consciousness with the wellspring of the abundance you seek, not more "stuff."

The greatest barrier to witnessing the manifestation of your positive energies reflected back to you is your belief in separation. Embracing oneness with Spirit and all people is a vital part of successfully manifesting your dreams. The ubiquitous belief that we are separate from our Creator—and He, being a temperamental patriarch, blesses or curses us with the conditions in our lives—lowers our consciousness and attracts chaos. Backward beliefs like these stem from fear-based interpretations of divine wisdom. Many still think that God will take care of them when they behave and think as required by His jealous, scorekeeping nature. If this is true, then it must also be true that the millions of suffering children around the world have done some horrible things to warrant the lives they are forced to endure. Few of us consciously agree with this, yet so many still pray for the Infinite to stop doing certain things and start doing others. Our Creator is doing what It has always done: being a force of infinite, unconditional, all-encompassing love and beauty. God is changeless, and not one beloved creation will be lost. What we call "life," many wisdom teachings call "illusion" or "sleep," which is a time when we become unconscious of our oneness with the Divine. Just as a child asleep in her family home may dream of being hurt, she will awake intact and unharmed. Though it may appear otherwise, beneath the illusions and appearances of human discord, we are safe in the eternal protection, love, and grace of the Divine.

Your dominant vibration, which is created by your innermost thoughts, beliefs, and feelings, brings you into or out of alignment with God's ever-flowing grace. Abundance, health, success, peace, and joy are everywhere and always have been. It is we who've been elsewhere. We must clean out our consciousness, cultivate the energy we wish to connect with, and make space in our lives for the good we seek.

Several years ago, I was faced with a legal matter, the outcome of which would dramatically affect my financial future. My home, my plans to send my children to school and college, and my ability to perform my responsibilities as a single mother were all on the line. The case was complex, far stranger than anything I'd studied in law school.

For the better part of a year, I had to attend court hearings where up to seven lawyers, each with a different agenda, argued for the outcome they wanted. Not one of them was wholly on my side. I was so afraid of the possibility of losing everything that over the course of the year I lost my center and succumbed to worry and doubt. I abandoned Spirit and relied on my intellect. I have a good mind and a gift for foresight and strategy, but with so many opposing, similarly adept minds I couldn't make any progress. One issue turned into several more, and it became painfully apparent that coming to any satisfactory resolution was unlikely. I grew to despise each lawyer. I hated them for accepting money to create issues and problems that would feed them for years while I suffered.

By the eighth hearing, I'd grown accustomed to showing up at court, watching the spectacle, praying that God would make the judge rule in my favor, feeling crushed when instead he continued the case until all the new issues could be examined, and finally imploding into an emotional mess in the backseat of my car. Bad got worse, and as one legal problem grew into several others, my anxiety and despair skyrocketed. I lost weight and spent the better part of several weeks in bed. There was no end in sight.

Then, one day, something profound happened inside of me. I gave in to love and let go. I released the fear of losing everything. I reminded myself that I was born with nothing, had risen from less than that as a welfare mom, and the same energies that had lifted me out of poverty would still be there for me if I had to start over. I surrendered to the love I knew existed for me and everyone else, including the judge and lawyers. For the first time in months, I felt no fear. That week, I attended a business conference and inadvertently ran straight into the presiding judge. He was startled, and he struggled to remember where he had met me. I introduced myself, and he immediately realized that ethically he couldn't speak to me. He stammered and ran off. I sent him love as I watched him go.

Nothing in the outside world had changed, but inside I was free. I showed up at court for the next hearing full of peace, knowing that the force that had created the universe loved me. I sat in the courtroom and for the first time, I saw the attorneys as people with families, dreams, struggles, and insecurities. I recognized that the

Infinite loved them into existence, and I silently wished each of them wellness and peace.

The morning began as usual with the lawyers commencing an irreconcilable discussion, but this time the judge interrupted. He explained that he'd run into me in public and then consulted a senior judge to confirm that no ethical standards had been compromised. What he said next nearly brought me to the floor. He looked across the courtroom and announced that the case had gone on for too long, and that it was time that I got on with my life. In an instant, he ruled, settling every aspect of the case in a very fair way and closing it, right there. I stood transfixed, rooted to the floor. I must have looked stunned, because one of the attorneys asked me if I was okay. I couldn't answer. I was trying to fit my mind around the clear lesson I'd learned. When I made ego the God of my life, I was small, powerless, ineffective, and alone. When I came into court armed only with divine love and no expectations, I left free, provided for, and safe. The moment I surrendered my fear, worry, doubt, and anger, and gave over my reliance on intellect and strategy to trusting Source, everything changed. To this day, I am not sure exactly what happened. Did my chance run-in with the judge and his ensuing discussion with a senior judge help him come to a conclusion in my case? I don't know. What I do know is that universal love is the most powerful force in existence and it will use anything and anyone to bring light into a situation.

Open your heart to love for yourself, God, and all people, no matter how they appear. Let go of negativity, resentment, and feeling like a victim. Let love rule your life, and the world will unfurl at your feet.

44

CONCEIVE YOUR DREAM

A Goddess fixes her gaze and the world reflects her image.

Women are masters of creation. The first and most important part of conceiving a dream is going deep within to discover what you really want. As you explore, you'll first bump into ideas you may think are your dreams. They aren't. Often the first layer is populated by old ideas implanted by society and the people who raised you. Go deeper. The question is: If all things were possible, what would you want to be, do, and have during your very short stay on the planet?

Answer in broad strokes, first. What kind of career, family, health, finances, relationships, leisure, and spiritual life do you want to have? Would your answers be the same if no one ever saw you living this way? When you picture yourself living a totally fulfilled life, do you feel lighter and inspired? The right dream is one that calls up a powerful *"Yes"* response in your body. For me, there is a blissful sensation in the pit of my belly, which is the same place that goes haywire when I'm acting in conflict with my intuition. I've come to trust that my higher self recognizes the path to my highest good, and I've learned to recognize its signals. When my thoughts are in alignment with my authentic dreams, I feel a strong and solid sense of authority and knowing in my center, and this propels me forward.

CREATING A VISION BOARD

When you are ready to refine your broad, generalized dreams into specific and clear visions, try creating a vision board. The process of making a vision board allows me to easily communicate with my higher self. I start with a piece of poster board or other such surface, then assemble several stacks of travel, inspirational, wedding, nature, and other magazines that feature beautiful images. I cut out anything that sparks my attention. I always end up with an enormous pile of clippings: these are potentials, possibilities to consider. Then I call on the Infinite, my highest good and higher self. I meditate holding the intention that I release my ego and surrender my will to the Divine. I open myself up and ask that I be guided toward the images that will lead to my highest good. From this centered place, I look through each photo in the entire stack of clippings, checking my center and honoring the feeling each image evokes. I let everything unfold without my conscious direction. When I'm finished, I have a stack of words and images that stir my core. Before I paste a single image to the board, I glue on writings that reflect the foundation I wish to build my vision upon.

My vision board of 2009 was pasted over the words "God for us, with us, and in us." Among the images was a picture of a group of bridesmaids that looked like sisters who loved each other. I was attracted to the image because I wanted more sisters in my life, and I wanted us to laugh together. I missed feeling connected to lots of positive women. In 2011, my wish came true in the most unexpected and fun way. My friend asked me to be a bridesmaid in her wedding, and she had eight wonderful, funny, and positive women for bridesmaids. The wedding was extravagant and entailed much preparation; we traveled to St. Martin and Chicago, and we had numerous rehearsals, lunches, and dinners together.

I fell in love with them, and it felt so good. I remember posing for photographs at the wedding and marveling at the prophetic picture on my vision board.

My board also had several pictures representing financial abundance: money falling from the sky and growing out of the ground, a beautiful home, and a new car. Images of free-flowing money serve as a reminder that abundance and wealth are neutral energies that take on the feeling tone of the individual. I love the freedom, comfort, and access that prosperity provides. I want this for myself, for you, and for all people. In my perfect world, all needs are met all of the time. This is the energy I cast on my finances.

As the nation's economy contracted, the effects of the mass consciousness of lack swept the country and overflowed, touching everyone, myself included. Although it was not always easy, I held fast to my perspective and beliefs, made smart decisions, and amplified my work efforts. I reinforced and affirmed my beliefs about money and opportunity being ever present and always available to me. I fared much better than those who were mentally and emotionally swept under by the tide of lack. The daily act of reinforcing the positive energy I had around money carried me through.

Next to a picture of a little girl (who reminded me of myself as a child), I pasted a picture of Michael Bernard Beckwith, my spiritual teacher and founder of the Agape International Spiritual Center. Michael played an integral part in my healing from the loss of my marriage, and I put him on my board because, to me, his face is synonymous with the ever-present opportunity to choose love, peace, joy, healing, and surrender. Whenever I see him, I am reminded that I am here on purpose and have important work to do. What I never imagined was that one day the head of Agape Media International's ("AMI") book publishing division would see my blog on an Internet site and approach me about writing this book. I love Michael, and to publish a book with his organization means the world to me.

This brings me to the image covering the bottom left corner of my vision board: a Roman goddess reclining in luxury as an attendant waves a feathered fan over her. I'd been exploring, embracing, and expanding the power of femininity within me for years. For me, this picture represents success and the idea that I can live the life I desire and embody the love, beauty, grace, strength, and vulnerabilities of the Divine Feminine. This image shows her as a fully expressed woman, relaxed and peaceful. At the time, I had no plan to write this book. I had just finished my memoir and wanted to publish it first. When AMI approached me, something inside me lit up. Venus seemed to awaken and jump right off my vision board.

Finally, the phrase "Not taking risks is risky" covered a couple of inches on the board. At the time, I didn't know why I'd placed these words on the board. It seemed such an obvious statement and unnecessary, but I've learned not to argue with my higher self. Before I agreed to take my attention away from my memoir and start writing *Resurrecting Venus*, I spent a few weeks thinking about whether I was ready. I have always placed high expectations on myself. Before I agree to take on a project, I need to know that my motives are based in loving, that I can deliver more than enough, and that the results will benefit at least one other person, ideally many. I felt that I could easily satisfy these criteria, but something held me back.

In time, the truth emerged. I knew that writing another book would take a year of my life, and time away from other opportunities and activities. Most importantly, writing this book would cause me to risk failure. Failure doesn't exist unless a person quits—it's a learning experience that gives feedback, and so long as we get back up and move forward, success is inevitable. Yes, I know, but a part of me felt intimidated and afraid to risk it. In that moment, the words on my vision board made sense. I had placed them there for my future self. I needed to see it plainly written before me. So keep this in mind:

> Risks: take them. Mistakes: don't be afraid to make them. Dreams: reach for them. Love: fall for it. Life is too short to tether oneself to the illusory safety of mediocrity; no poison kills more slowly or painfully than regret.

Not taking risks is risky, but the real risk is failing to risk anything.

When constructed with the help of your higher self, vision boards are a powerful resource to support your dreams. Whether the images create the reality, reflect a deeper knowing, or influence what you focus on and, thus, create it (or all three) doesn't matter. Make your own vision board and be grateful for the gifts it can give. You can see my board on my website (http://CynthiaOccelli.com).

When making and using your board, be choosy about who sees it before your dreams come to fruition. Dreams are like embryos, they need constant nourishment and protection if they are going to be born and survive. I rarely share my board or dreams with anyone outside of my closest confidants, who I know will not judge or criticize them. Let the energy of creation build and accumulate around your heart's desires. When you share your dreams for no reason other than to include someone else, you run the risk of diluting vital energy or even cutting off the flow. If they share their fears, doubts, and limiting beliefs with you, they may inadvertently derail your confidence. That said, I have found it beneficial to share my vision with one absolutely committed fan. This person can be anyone, so long as they are fiercely supportive of you and willing to hold the space for your highest good. I share my dreams with one person who has an unshakable belief in me and desires my success. I do this because I know that I will not always feel strong and confident. If I get discouraged or my vision weakens, this person is still holding my vision and supporting me. Everything we create exists first in the mind. I want my dreams to always be alive in at least one mind other than mine.

A final note, sometimes you may put something on the board that doesn't match up to what you choose in life. That's perfectly okay. We are ever-changing beings. For example, I put a specific car on my board. I'd test driven it and selected the color, options, and terms. As my financial and life situation fell in to place, I took notice of the car whenever I saw one on the road. When the day finally came to buy the car, I called the salesman and made the preliminary arrangements to purchase it. On my way to the dealership, I noticed an entirely different brand of car (in a color I thought I'd never buy) sitting on the showroom floor in an expensive area of town. I stopped just to have a look and because I wanted to prove to myself that the car shown on my board was far superior. I sat in the showroom car and really liked it! The fleet manager happened to be on the floor and—to make an effortless and fun story short—I bought the car. I got a better deal and I absolutely adore driving it. So be open to things turning out differently and more satisfying than you first expected.

45

TWO TEMPLES OF VENUS

*A masterwork of Creation unrivaled in its splendor
demands an atmosphere worthy of the Divine.*

THE FIRST TEMPLE: YOUR BODY

The two Temples of Venus are your body and your sacred living
spaces. The first temple, your body, is the residence of your soul.
When seen for what it is, the blessing of your body becomes
exquisitely clear. Your body, right now, is absolutely magnificent.
It gives you all of its effort and energy and works 24 hours a day
for your entire lifetime. No other being will serve you this way.
Love and appreciate your body just the way it is. Join forces with
your body; be grateful for its service and devotion to you and
protect it from harm. Your body is not a barrier, nor an enemy or
object to criticize or burden with shame. It's a divinely created
vessel with powerful capacities to create, love, express, and heal, so
celebrate your beautiful body.

Turn away from the malicious manipulation and degradation
the female body has suffered from advertisers and the media. They
have one motivation: to make you feel inadequate and insecure
so that you will spend money on products, surgeries, and drugs
to "fix" yourself.

Falling for this propaganda is like toweling off in a rainstorm and expecting to get dry. Instead, take shelter in the truth: your body is innately and inherently beautiful. Forget taking your beauty cues from smarmy marketers, and let the masters of beauty set you straight. Do an online search for paintings by Sandro Botticelli, William Bouguereau, and Alexandre Cabanel, all bearing the title *The Birth of Venus*, and Titian's *Venus of Urbino*, and let the refined eyes of the artistic masters enlighten you. Venus, as painted by these outstanding artists, is shapely; she has hips, thighs, breasts, and full arms. Her belly is soft. She is healthy, not obese, and not anorexic. Her various representations reflect the fantasy of a sublimely beautiful woman and bear much similarity. Even when painted in the glow of celestial splendor, Venus, as represented in these images, sets a far more attainable standard of bodily beauty than today's Photoshopped skeletons.

Your conditioned mind may attempt to dismiss these representations as outdated standards of beauty, but changes in the standard are created by commercialism, not a shift in what men desire. If you are ever fortunate enough to stand before one of the paintings mentioned above, peel your gaze from the glory of Venus and spy the men watching her. Observe their mesmerized eyes as they sweep her entirety, then longingly linger. Some men remain perfectly still for several minutes, losing themselves in the dream of being loved by her. Men love women, real women. The changing beauty standard toward women is about money, not about men. Find some paintings of the same period depicting males, when you're finished man-watching. Notice that the standards for the ideal male figure haven't changed. If you happen to be in Florence, ask yourself what woman wouldn't want to be carried to her bath by Michelangelo's David? Wonderfully, women have a far greater likelihood of maintaining a body like Venus than men do of embodying David.

The motivation for tending to your body must be for your own pleasure and satisfaction. Natural physical beauty is synonymous with true health. You must be able to rely on your body to carry you through life's joys and struggles without physical pain, illness, or premature fatigue. Two-thirds of Americans are overweight or obese, when measured against the Body Mass Index. At the same time, diet books and foods and weight-loss programs abound. Here again, the root of the problem stems from commercialism. Mixed messages attached to harmful products are everywhere. There are vitamin-fortified, sugary sparkling beverages with antioxidants thrown in to confuse you into thinking they are healthy. Bisphenol A (BPA), the chemical used in the lining of up to 92 percent of canned goods, from soups to baby formula, is linked to obesity, cancer, and insulin resistance. You cannot rely on food producers, retailers, packaging manufacturers, cosmetics companies, or the Food and Drug Administration to protect you from harmful foods and products. You must take responsibility for the safety and quality of everything you put in your mouth and on your body. Concentrated Animal Feeding Operation (CAFO) meat, pesticides, BPA, hydrogenated oils, excess and harmful sugars, preservatives, parabens, and a litany of cancer-linked chemicals are now common in our food, other products, and the environment; and this is just a sampling of harmful concerns.

To figure out how and what to eat for great health, a happy weight, and sensual satisfaction is a daunting task. Our current approach to weight loss and maintenance—calorie restriction, deprivation, strange combinations of foods, diet drinks, refined carbohydrates, and prepackaged items—poison our bodies and result in greater weight gain later. Thank heaven for one saving grace: our great-grandmothers.

Reaching down through the centuries, our great-grandmothers still are able to take care of us. They knew the secrets to vibrant health; they may have been unable to detail the science supporting their knowledge, but they were wiser than any diet guru. Their wisdom was based on two fundamental principles: eat to live, and food is medicine. Most foods were consumed whole, meaning in or close to their naturally grown state. Fruits and vegetables with wild fish, farm-raised proteins or nuts, and small amounts of whole grains were staples. Sugary treats such as home-baked cakes and cookies were less processed and eaten only to mark special occasions. Packaged and fast food didn't exist. Breakfast, the meal that sets the stage for the day, was substantial. Lunch was good-sized and provided sufficient fuel to carry the family through to dinner, the smallest meal of the day. The seasons ruled the table, which meant lots of fruit in the summer, and kale and cabbage in the winter. Whatever is available at your local farmers' market is what great-grandma would have eaten.

Our ancestors' medicines of chicken soup for a cold, chamomile tea for an upset stomach, and lemon with honey for a cough have all been proven effective by science. Their rates of cancer, heart disease, and diabetes were dramatically lower than ours. In their time, the majority of the population would easily have fit into the healthy BMI range. We can use our great-grandmother's innate wisdom to keep a body that is naturally a healthy weight.

[NOTE: If you don't like vegetables (I thought I hated them), chances are you haven't learned to prepare them well. I have yet to meet a vegetable hater, child or adult, who can turn down my kale salad or brussels sprouts. It is well worth learning how to prepare properly cooked, deliciously seasoned vegetables.]

As feminine women, we know everything worth doing must be done in the most pleasurable way, weight loss included. If you have a lot of (or even a little) weight to lose, never starve or deprive yourself. Deprivation is neither pleasant, nor enjoyable. It only sets you up to fail. How can anyone be expected to adhere to a lifestyle that makes her feel unhappy? No matter how much discipline you have, your sense of lack will outlive it. So let's strike the D-word forever and shift our focus to abundance.

Whatever you place your focus on grows. Focus on your weight and watch it increase. This is likely the antithesis of your goal. Instead of focusing on your terrible eating habits and the dangers in the food supply, choose abundance: add five or more servings of fresh or frozen, organic fruits and vegetables to your diet every day; you can have as much as you want. The following week, add two servings of fresh, sustainably caught fish to your repertoire. The next week, switch to pastured meats and eggs. Then focus on meal sizes: largest in the morning to smallest in the evening. Next, switch to whole grains and use them as side dishes to your vegetable entrées. Relax and pay attention to the love, respect, and support you are giving your body.

Over time, a few things will happen. You will begin to purchase and prepare fresh foods automatically. You'll develop a taste for the new foods you're eating. The fiber in the whole foods will fill you up faster. Your cravings will lessen as your body obtains the nutrition it needs. In time, the new life-giving foods will edge out the old unhealthy ones. Your skin will clear, your hair will become shinier, and your eyes will look brighter. Your mood will improve and smooth to an even keel. Vibrant energy will emerge and remain. For me, about two months after adding a serving a day of cruciferous vegetables (broccoli, cabbage, and kale) to my meals, I experienced a welcome reduction in mood swings and headaches associated with PMS. Food really is medicine. If you want to learn about the wonders and benefits of food, look for books that focus on natural health and wellness, and avoid diet books and eating plans.

Exercise is an important and required component of real health. The most important aspect of your choice in exercise is its genuine appeal to you. If you like what you're doing, you'll show up again tomorrow. Nothing is more important. My mother absolutely despises exercise. She's had a long career in accounting and spends hours and hours seated at her desk. She played no sports as a child and has no interest in exercise. When I was young, I remember watching her force herself to attend aerobic classes daily for a week or two, having a miserable time, and then quitting—until she forgot how much she hated it and started over!

Over the years, I encouraged her to try different workouts, start walking, and join the gym. We both ended up frustrated. Finally, I quit pushing. After many years without exercising, my mom decided that she wanted to check out a level-one class at the yoga studio where I practice. I went with her to the first couple of classes, but then my schedule prevented me from going for a while. To my thrilled surprise, my mom went without me and continued to take a class three times a week consistently, without any prodding from me. She had finally found a form of exercise she enjoyed. She is now stronger, more toned, no longer stiff, and making new friends.

THE LESSON: If you think you don't like exercise, keep looking. Keep trying different methods. Finding the right form of exercise heightens your enjoyment and well-being. Keep trying new kinds of exercise, new teachers, and new gyms or classes until you find something that matches the needs and abilities of your body.

THE SECOND TEMPLE OF VENUS: YOUR HOME

Your living space, your environment, is vital to creating a nurturing, fulfilling, and joyous life. Women are innately sensual. What we experience in our world moves us; it touches our hearts, sways our feelings, and drives our emotions. We are extremely sensitive and vulnerable to chaotic or toxic environments. It doesn't cost a fortune to create an environment worthy of your grace. Small adjustments can create massive shifts in your sense of peace, security, mood, and romantic desires.

You know what you like, but do you make it a part of your environment? Do you dream of going to Italy? Is something you love about Italy reflected in your home? Are your surroundings comfortable, uncluttered, and inviting? If not, consider the message this sends to your inner being and to anyone who visits you. Get conscious about the items, colors, and textures that surround you. Choose tones, fabrics, and music to nurture the Goddess in you. It's not okay to skimp on yourself, because it reinforces the idea that your needs and wants aren't important. Send yourself a message that you are worthy of attention, adoration, and comfort, and watch your inner being transform your outer experience.

One of the most powerful actions a woman can perform as she prepares to resurrect her Venus is to do a thorough housecleaning. Go through every drawer, cabinet, closet, and cupboard. If you haven't used something in a year, give it away, throw it away, or repurpose it. This will open the flow and allow new and beneficial things to come to you.

Organize what you decide to keep and make your space aesthetically beautiful and fit for a Goddess. Don't underestimate the power of placing a beautiful flower on your desk, hanging a painting of paradise on your wall, or playing the movie soundtrack of *Dangerous Beauty* in the background. I could not have written this book without them.

46

WHAT WOULD CLEOPATRA DO?

Take up your crown, scepter, and robe;
your Queendom awaits your ascent to the throne.

I chose to end this book with writing devoted to Cleopatra because, in my opinion, she is the finest example of the fullest expression of feminine power. Cleopatra was a queen, mother, leader of an empire, and lover, who lived first for herself and then for her people. Shape-shifting into whatever form was necessary, she was able to nurture her children, protect her interests, advance her desires, and create beauty. Seductress, negotiator, tradeswoman, entertainer, hostess, and warrior, she created what she desired.

Believing she was a descendant of Isis, the Egyptian Goddess of motherhood, nature, magic, and fertility, Cleopatra never felt she was inadequate or unworthy. She envied no one and believed herself worthy of every wonderful gift life could offer. Set to live out the divine traits of Isis, she practiced compassion and concern for her subjects. When others betrayed her, she methodically took the actions necessary to protect herself and her people from harm, but she didn't revel in bloodshed. Though she is portrayed as a stunning physical specimen, one of the most remarkable and noteworthy testaments to the power of personality is that (according to historians) she was mildly attractive, at best. They credit her wit, humor, and pleasing voice with the magic that charmed beggars and statesmen alike to fall in love with her.

The next time you're faced with a decision you're unsure about, ask yourself: *What would Cleopatra do?* Let the answer come to you. The point in asking this question is not to encourage you to disconnect from reality and fantasize about ordering a ship to make preparation for a Nile voyage. It's far more powerful than that.

Aligning yourself with a powerful archetype—it doesn't have to be Cleopatra; pick one that inspires you—may seem, at first, like playing pretend, but the results will be anything but imaginary. Assume your place on the throne. Your life is your Queendom, and the voices in your mind are your subjects. Rule them. Your lover, children, relatives, friends, and community are your royal family. Together, you rule the world with compassion. Get clear on what you want from your life and prepare to receive it. Hold the vision of yourself as the adored queen that you are, and carry her energy with you. The world will see you the way you see yourself.

Let's explore some real-life applications for modern women:

SCENARIO #1:

Connie has spent a week working hard on a new project. She's finally finished and in need of rest and rejuvenation. She arrives home, and just as she's settling in, her daughter asks if a couple of girlfriends can spend the night. Exhausted, but feeling guilty for wanting to say "No," Connie can't decide what to do. What would Cleopatra do?

Cleopatra would see the bigger picture. She would recognize that the welfare of the royal family rests upon her ability to govern from the throne (complete her projects at work). If she fails to take the time to rest and restore her energy, the whole queendom (the quality of her life) might be at risk. Cleopatra would ask her daughter to postpone the sleepover or, provided the girlfriend's family checks out, move it to her house instead.

SCENARIO #2:

Diana met Scott, who could be the man of her dreams, two weeks ago at a museum. After their last sublime date, Scott said he'd call her in the morning. Three days have passed. Diana wonders what happened. She wants to call Scott and get to the bottom of it. What would Cleopatra do?

The idea of a queen chasing after a man who doesn't have the decency to follow through on his word—or at least explain why he's choosing not to—is preposterous. Suitors are like grapes: another bunch will show up with dinner.

SCENARIO #3:

Ashley is sitting with a group of girlfriends who start gossiping about a common acquaintance. Ashley knows much about the story, and she is tempted to join in the conversation and share the juicy bits she knows. What would Cleopatra do?

Cleopatra understands the value and importance of her reputation and the fact that she never knows when she may need an ally. She would neither wish to be lowered by another, nor participate in the diminishing of someone who is not present to defend his position. Cleopatra would refrain from risking her own reputation by sullying the reputation of another.

SCENARIO #4:

Beatrix moves into a new home. Life is busy, and she considers getting the rest of the family moved in and situated, and *then* making her own space comfortable. What would Cleopatra do?

As queen, matriarch, and goddess, Cleopatra would see to it that her quarters were made beautiful and comfortable immediately. She would recognize the importance of preserving herself, as the queen and ruler of her empire, and creating the environment most conducive to her happiness first—because a happy woman creates happiness for all.

SCENARIO #5:

Anna wrote a song. She discovers that her former business partner, Steve, has published it, and is taking the credit and the money. Anna confronts Steve, and he tells her tough luck. Steve feels entitled to the song because it was created while they were in business together. Anna is devastated. Her feelings are hurt, and she knows the song belongs to her. What would Cleopatra do?

Cleopatra knows that when intense emotion is at play, a pause is in order. She would wait a few hours, days, or weeks. When the emotional energy subsided and her mind, body, and spirit were calm, she would consider her options. From a place of centeredness, she'd make the best choice for herself without regard for Steve or his feelings, and employ the fortitude to see it through. If she decided to attack, in this case to sue Steve, she would use the masculine tools of decisive assertiveness to obtain justice.

Seeing your life through the eyes of a noble queen elevates the level of care you give yourself and enhances the way you treat others. Ask yourself, *What would Cleopatra do?* A master tactician with her eye steadily fixed on the greatest good, Cleopatra would advise you to make decisions that honor your heart, your being, and your responsibilities.

AFTERWORD

VENUS RISING

Unearthed from the ruins, restored and alive,
Venus is resurrected and all of life thrives.

May this book become a beloved companion that will encourage, inspire, and support you in co-creating with Spirit the love, work, family, and creative expression you were born to live. Every major life change consists of a series of smaller ones. Go slowly. Treat yourself the way you would a child learning to walk. Kindly, gently, ease yourself toward the truest expression of your magnificence. Embrace every ounce of your womanly goodness, treasure every loving thought, and honor the Goddess you are. The graces of beauty, compassion, balancing wisdom, and joy ascend only through a receptive heart. Your pleasure, happiness, and creative expression call it forth.

Make way, my sister; Venus is rising.

Love,

Cynthia

SUGGESTED RESOURCES

BOOKS

The Memoirs of Cleopatra, by Margaret George
An epic story of Cleopatra's life, loves, power, and pain, this delicious adventure will make your heart ache, swoon, and sing. I recommend listening to the audio book.

Ina May's Guide to Childbirth, by Ina May Gaskin
Written by the "mother of midwifery," this book offers a comprehensive understanding of the benefits of natural birth and the many ways to reduce or eliminate pain during delivery.

Mama Glow: A Guide to Your Fabulous Abundant Pregnancy,
by Latham Thomas
Drawing on yoga, vegan nutrition, and our body's innate wisdom, Latham Thomas lovingly guides women on the journey to motherhood.

Why Gender Matters: What Parents and Teachers Need to Know about the Emerging Science of Sex Differences, by Leonard Sax
This eye-opening book will leave you saying, "Finally, it all makes sense." If you have children, do them a favor and read it.

Boys and Girls Learn Differently! by Michael Gurian and Patricia Henley, with Terry Trueman
This wonderful book demystifies gender learning differences

and empowers parents and teachers to help boys and girl thrive socially and academically.

Women Don't Ask: The High Cost of Avoiding Negotiation—and Positive Strategies for Change, by Linda Babcock and Sara Laschever
This is an important resource for all women, in work and in life.

FILM

Dangerous Beauty, Warner Bros.
This sumptuous and beautiful film will wake your inner Venus.

The Business of Being Born, produced by Ricki Lake.
This important film is a must for any woman contemplating child-bearing. www.thebusinessofbeingborn.com

Orgasmic Birth, by Debra Pascali-Bonaro, www.orgasmicbirth.com

AUDIO

Inside-Out Wellness, Wayne W. Dyer, Christiane Northrup, 2009.
This fantastic audio recording explores how to face our fears and use pleasure as a means of creating the lives we desire. Pay close attention for Christiane Northrup's explanation of the power of nitric oxide.

Dangerous Beauty: Original Motion Picture Score, by George Fenton
Beautiful, romantic and delightful.

TranscenDance, by Michael Bernard Beckwith
This soul-awakening CD combines great music with words that motivate, inspire, and shine light on negativity.

JOIN US

Come learn, share, and be embraced by your sisters.

www.ResurrectingVenus.com

www.facebook.com/LIFEblog

www.twitter.com/CynthiaOccelli

www.YouTube.com/CynthiaOccelli

Listen for Cynthia Occelli on Hay House Radio
www.hayhouseradio.com

ABOUT THE AUTHOR

I'm an avid reader of personal development books, and I credit much of my success to their wisdom. Yet I'd often wondered whether a book's writer really lived the teachings they espoused. I was fortunate to have the opportunity to interact with a few popular authors in private settings. I discovered that they're not super-human; they're just people, like me.

I've chosen to take this space, and instead of trying to impress you with my achievements, give you a peek into the unfiltered me, so that you'll know that I am human—just like you.

Not every day is a wonderful day for me. Sometimes, I'm tired, anxious, and impatient or have no interest in seeing another human being. I am not a perfect mother, daughter, lover, or friend, but I do my best. I cry, I get angry, and on occasion the world gets the best of me and I take a soak in victimhood. Blessedly, these moments are increasingly rare. I read my own books and blogs and strive to always walk my talk. I make mistakes and I fail. I'm not perfect, but I like me.

I'm a very friendly introvert. I love people intensely, but if there's a crowd, chances are good that I won't be in it. I speak publicly—not because I enjoy it, but because I feel compelled.

My burning desire is to significantly improve the lives of as many people as possible. It's my way of transmuting loss and tragedy into love; I call it the alchemy of pain.

I have a man who loves me the way every woman deserves to be loved (yes, just the way I described in "Venus in Love"). My children are the light of my life. I am fiercely independent and very attached to my mother. I've had the same best friend since I was 12. I'd lay my life down for any one of them.

I love animals, and because I often work in my pajamas and wear them to pick up my daughter, you may well see me flailing about in the streets of Los Angeles trying to catch a shrew (my last rescue actually was a shrew, I named him Percy) and looking more like Sasquatch than Venus.

I am the most powerful person in my life, and on most days I wake up surrounded by beauty and filled with passion and love. It was not always this way. I am finally free, at home in my skin, and happier than ever before. My promise to you is this: I've built my life around the ideas contained in this book. They work. Take them and make them yours.

With love,

Cynthia

Other Offerings from
Agape Media Artists & Authors

Agape Media International (AMI) is dedicated to promoting artists and art forms that uplift the human spirit and inspiring individuals to contribute their own talents to the creation of a world that works for everyone.

BOOKS

Michael Bernard Beckwith | *TranscenDance Expanded*

Michael Bernard Beckwith | *The Answer Is You–Heart Sets & Mind Sets for Self-Discovery*

Michael Bernard Beckwith | *40-Day Mind Fast Soul Feast*

Michael Bernard Beckwith | *Life Visioning–A Transformative Process for Activating Your Unique Gifts and Highest Potential*

Michael Bernard Beckwith | *Spiritual Liberation–Fulfilling Your Soul's Potential*

Dianne Burnett | *The Road to Reality–Voted Off the Island! …My Journey As A Real-Life Survivor*

Charles Holt | *Intuitive Rebel–Tuning in to the Voice that Matters*

Carl Studna | *Click!–Choosing Love One Frame at a Time*

AUDIO PROGRAMS BY MICHAEL BERNARD BECKWITH

The Life Visioning Process
The Life Visioning Life Visioning Kit
The Rhythm of a Descended Master
Your Soul's Evolution
Living from the Overflow
Spiritual Liberation Audio Book
Life Visioning Audio Book

DVDs

The Answer Is You—PBS Special
Spiritual Liberation, the Movie
Supewise Me!—The Law of the Heart
Living in the Revelation

MUSIC CDS

Music from the PBS Special—The Answer Is You
feat. Will.I.Am, Siedah Garrett, Niki Haris, Rickie Byars Beckwith,
Agape International Choir
Jami Lula & Spirit in the House / *There's a Healin' Goin' On*
Charles Holt | *I Am*
Charles Holt | *Rushing Over Me*
Rickie Byars Beckwith | *Supreme Inspiration*
Ester Nicholson | *Child Above the Sun*
Ben Dowling | *The Path of Peace*
Michael Bernard Beckwith | *TranscenDance*

INSPIRATIONAL CARDS
Life Lift-Off Cards

Agape Media International

www.agapeme.com

For more information regarding Agape International Spiritual Center
in Los Angeles, visit **www.agapelive.com**

NOTES